i

# A GENTLE GIANT

# A GENTLE GIANT

## The life of Blessing Kawanzaruwa, 1954-2017

Foreword by Dr Gallie Kawanzaruwa

All proceeds go to the BK Foundation

*To Blessing, for a life well lived and very well worth sharing; to all those whose lives he touched with his love; and to the children and orphans of Zimbabwe, in the hope they too can experience the opportunities he and his wife enjoyed.*

# TABLE OF CONTENTS

FOREWORD ................................................................................................. x

CHAPTER 1: MY FAMILY ......................................................................... 1

My childhood ............................................................................................ 2

My great grandfather.............................................................................. 3

My mother................................................................................................. 4

Ode to Maria, the Merry Matriarch................................................ 13

My sister, Phoebe ................................................................................. 14

My wife, Gallie ...................................................................................... 17

CHAPTER 2: EDUCATION IN TROUBLED ZIMBABWE ............... 25

The coming of the white man ........................................................... 27

Self-rule ................................................................................................... 28

Education, the secret of our success............................................... 28

Education and politics in Zimbabwe............................................ 34

Life at Mazowe .................................................................................... 35

Becoming a teacher ............................................................................ 37

The Henderson experience............................................................... 39

My last days at Henderson ........................................................... 44

A new home............................................................................................ 44

St Manocks and Kutsaga Research Station School....................... 46

CHAPTER 3: SETTLING IN THE UNITED KINGDOM................... 51

My first experiences in Sunderland ............................................... 54

The Leazes .................................................................................59

The prophecy became real ............................................................61

CHAPTER 4: THE UAE AND DECLINING HEALTH .......................63

Al Ain.......................................................................................64

The Emirate of Ras Al Khaimah.......................................................66

Fujairah....................................................................................67

CHAPTER 5: LOOKING BACK ON MY LIFE ...............................69

Political philosophy ....................................................................73

EPILOGUE: BLESSING PROMOTED TO GLORY..........................75

REFERENCES.............................................................................77

# FOREWORD

I am writing this foreword as a widow. My husband, Blessing Kawanzaruwa, passed away on 14 April 2017, while in the final stages of his memoirs. They describe his many struggles in obtaining an education, before going on to succeed in life. I am very passionate about publishing his story: it is well worth telling and sets out what we shared for 36 years of marriage. The life we shared together had so many happy memories and blessings, they entirely surpass any hardships or challenges we faced.

Of course I am grieved to have lost a soulmate - grief that will not go away easily for many years to come - but I also count myself so lucky to have shared a life with such a wise and amazing man, a father to my beautiful children and a gentle giant.

Blessing Kawanzaruwa was born in Mount Darwin, Zimbabwe, in 1954. He was seventh of a family of eight children. A devout Christian, he was born and raised in the Salvation Army. He trained as a teacher at Waddilove Teachers' College: triggering a 25-year career (five years of which were spent as a Deputy Headmaster) in teaching, before moving to the UK. He always believed that education was the way out of poverty and a path to success.

As you will read, his life was not always a bed of roses. He went through great hardship to obtain his education, from sewing other pupils' school shoes to help pay his tuition fees, to staying behind during school holidays and working for his school to raise enough money for his upkeep. This adversity made him especially passionate about education. Blessing went on to ensure that children who could not afford school fees (both from the local community and among our relatives) were given the opportunity by paying for them too.

Later, he moved to Sunderland, to join me and our children. He attended the University of Sunderland, where he graduated with a Master's in Gender, Culture and Development. He went on to study for another Master's in Special Needs and Inclusive Education; and a Diploma as a Personal Adviser at the University of Huddersfield.

He continued to influence the lives of children in both the UK and Zimbabwe. Blessing worked with vulnerable young people as a Personal Adviser and Activities Coordinator for Connexions: which made him fully appreciate that the vulnerability of young people, especially in education, is a universal concern.

Blessing had a lifelong dream of educating the less privileged in society - and was in the process of converting his private residence in Zimbabwe into a school (the BK Academy) before suddenly passing away. The BK Foundation was started in memory of this great man: whose passion for education will remain his legacy for generations to come.

The Foundation's main objectives are to raise funds, meaning that Blessing's work educating disadvantaged children will continue. It also aims to develop a scholarship programme, to help young people who cannot otherwise afford to go to school; and fully equip the BK Academy, which I have completed, with modern, state of the art facilities and resources.

The target is to open the new school in 2020. It will be fee-paying for those who can afford it; but free to orphans able to access it in Harare. The money raised from the school will, in turn, fund the education of orphans in rural Zimbabwe.

Africa's future depends on education. More children than ever are going to school, but tens of millions of Africans are still not obtaining an education. Fixing the problem will require billions of dollars of investment – and while our Academy won't be able to raise such sums, we can remedy this epidemic 'one child at a time' through our sponsorship programme.

With as little as 10 US dollars per month, we can change the life of a young person in Zimbabwe. At present, the future of many of these children is meaningless after primary school – but the BK Foundation says 'NO!' These children can enjoy the benefits of education through sponsorship. A future free from poverty is what we greatly desire for all of them. Philippians 4:19 NIV[19]: *'And my God will meet all your needs according to the riches of his glory in Christ'.*

The proceeds from sales of Blessing's book will also go towards this worthy venture. As his widow, and CEO of the Foundation, I am deeply committed to this philanthropic mission: which can put smiles on the faces of and give a real future so many children in Zimbabwe. At present, I am the BK Academy's major funder and sponsor. I will always be inspired by the struggles and vision of my late husband. Our mission now is to put his vision into transformative action.

Deuteronomy 10:18 NIV: *'He defends the cause of the fatherless and the widow, and loves the foreigner residing among you, giving them food and clothing'.* James 1:27 NIV (27): *'Religion that God our Father accepts as pure and faultless is this: to look after orphans and widows in their distress and to keep oneself from being polluted by the world'.* Genesis (ERV) 35:16-18: *'I have to live for Benjamin like Jacob after Rachael's death. The pains of Rachael at Benjamin's birth and ultimate death gave Jacob something to live for'.*

The BK Foundation will preserve and build upon the legacy of a special, unique man; a much missed, truly gentle giant, who touched the lives of so many, and continues to do so after his passing.

Dr Gallie Kawanzaruwa
CEO, BK Foundation.

# CHAPTER 1:

# MY FAMILY

In any family, support and stability can produce hugely positive results. I've been fortunate enough to be part of a stable family throughout my life: which has provided many important lessons. Sometimes, we have to walk away from something if we are to move forward. This is especially true with work: the world does not end if the manager says, 'You're fired'. Actually, this is only the start of the journey to success: as long as we retain the determination and zeal to challenge ourselves and grow along the way.

In writing this personal story, I want to record a history for my family, especially my three children and my wife. Some of the memories I set out may be saddening to read. Yet any given testimony is important and features a great deal to reflect on. However, for those who fail to keep a record, their priceless family histories disappear into the midst of time.

Recent developments in psychology and the social sciences have drawn attention to the significance of storytelling and narrative as a primary means of making sense of social experience and communicating with others (McLeod, 2001). Narrativity leads events and lives to be affirmed as being worth telling and thus, worth living. Stories give legibility; according to Frank (2002:3), when lives are shaped as narratives, 'they come from somewhere and are going somewhere... narratives do not seek self-fulfilment but address important social issues'.

## My childhood

Born into an extended family, where patriarchy was a form of governance, I grew up in a male-dominated environment. I was socialised in a system where I was constantly reminded that a man was always a hunter, an achiever and a conqueror. To be counted as a 'real man', my father always told me I had to have a family. Any man who fell short of this was considered weak.

Like my brothers, I was a revered son in a patient, tolerant, conservative - yet flexible, accommodating society (Achebe, 1959). There was a clear distinction between me and my sisters: who were raised to be future wives and drive the family's finances through the customary bridal price. It was my mother's role to nurture her daughters for their future roles as wives; in consequence of which, my brothers and I differed greatly from our sisters in our roles. For example, going to school was not necessary for them, for the simple reason that they did not need 'book education' (according to my society's cultural perspectives at the time).

This mindset is highlighted in *Nervous Conditions*, where the Zimbabwean novelist, Dangarembwa, depicts the plight of girls in colonial Rhodesia. Tambudzai, the girl in the novel, is refused education by her father: who provides the rejoinder that she will not 'cook books' and feed them to the husband.

Having himself obtained very limited reading and writing skills, my father recognised the importance of education: to some extent, at least. He therefore allowed some of my sisters to attend school, so they could read the Bible, just as he could. For the boys, the policy was different. We had to get a formal education and compete strongly with others in a country with very negative education policies for its indigenous population. Even then, the emphasis of our society remained on masculinity; it was my father's duty to train me into a fearless hunter and achiever. He told us stories of triumph and bravery when we sat around an evening fire, sharing our meal. He would often talk about the differences between us as men and my sisters as women.

Thus, we were not allowed to entertain a prolonged presence in the cooking house, in case we disturbed the girls as they helped our mother with household chores. Children grew up under a social structure which oversaw a clear division of labour. It's not that my sisters were exploited or oppressed; they simply had to fit in with their gendered roles at that time. My patriarchal upbringing had its advantages too: among them, protection of the young. We were protected by strangers, taboos and religious teachings from societal elders. Talking about sex was taboo, while saying anything ill against nature and the environment was 'punishable' by misfortunes in later life. For example, illness was thought of as punishment for disobedience.

Every boy in my village grew up in a protective society, where the environment yielded enough food and resources for learning and games. The ecosystem was pregnant with natural items for use. Before reaching my teens, I felt protected, nurtured and educated enough to live up to my father's expectations.

## My great grandfather

Our great grandfather, Chikowore, was a mysterious man who, according to legend, performed miracles. My mother told us numerous stories and adventures about him. My siblings and I would sit around a fire in my mother's kitchen hut during cold winter nights to listen to her stories. These were times to cherish; my mother was a master storyteller as she told us fables, myths and adventures involving our esteemed forbearers. The storytelling was, in most cases, accompanied by songs: some of which are still vivid in my mind even decades later.

One of my favourite stories was when the old man used to ask his own ancestors to provide food while out hunting. It is said that the food was provided only on a particular kind of tree: Muhacha. This practice, I later learnt, was not unique to my great grandfather; everyone during his era partook in it. The food was provided after a prayer to Musikavanhu (God). This was before the advent of the white man: whose missionary work brought the Bible into the locale.

As Christianity was introduced, these customs began to fade; undermined by new forms of prayer. This remains controversial to this very day: with many torn between African traditions and culture, while others have discarded them in favour of Christianity. This is what Nehanda and Kaguvi (our ancestral spirits) fought against when they were murdered. I will not go into detail on why and how this happened. I just want to set the scene of why some of our very important traditions were discarded with the advent of missionaries in Rhodesia and Nyasaland (now Zimbabwe).

My great grandfather also had a remarkable time managing the load he carried, especially after hunting and gathering many items of food: which he would, we might imagine, have needed help to carry home. I am told that he could make the load (such as bags of grain) move. He gave them names, and they could move once their names were called. The names were those of his children. As soon as he heard voices of people approaching, he would order the moving parcels to stop, which they did. If someone asked if he needed help to carry the load, he would say that his sons were on their way to help him. He is said to have performed many miracles, raising questions which none of the adults in my family could answer. The legend of my great grandfather even appears in written literature.

There is also a very strong belief in our clan that nobody should pay anyone back through evil. If somebody wrongs us, my great grandfather instructed that we should leave them alone - because if we pay them back, the person in question will encounter serious misfortune. I will not dwell on this, as many things remain mysterious to this day.

## My mother

My mother, Maria, was from the Nzou Katemavhu clan (Samanyanga) from Nyombwe. Her family stayed in the vicinity of Chibara Chinemanyika (Chawanda). After the death of her older brothers, she was born, and aptly named Hamukataye, meaning: 'You will not throw her away or bury her'. Maria's mother, Zunguzare, took her on her back from Chawanda. She was around 5 years old or possibly more, as she could remember some of the events which happened on the journey. She walked with her mother for days: crossing the Mazowe river, staying in caves and surviving on wild fruit and the hospitality of strangers. It is said that Mazowe River threw fish off its banks for them. Zunguzare took a big fish for food; the following day, people went with nets to the river and filled their sacks with fish.

Their journey took them to Pfungwe, where her brother was staying. Zunguzare stayed there with her brother for some time. Her husband, Chibvongodze Mvundura, was working for the white men on the farms. When Chibvongodze, Maria's father, went back to Nyombwe, he discovered that his wife had taken their child, and she had gone back to her people. Chibvongodze went to stay with his wife in Nyamaropa. Chibvongodze and Zunguzare had two more children, Berita and Eve, while in Nyamaropa. So Maria grew up living with her mother's people. When she was old enough, she met and married Latesi.

Maria was good at relating folklore and history to her children and grandchildren. She imparted wisdom and the value of family and relationships. She emphasised the latter; and taught us, her children, to live well with our relatives, who she loved very much.

She told us that during her journey with her mother, they were on a rocky outcrop overlooking a valley. They saw that a pride of lions had killed an animal. With an apparent death wish, Zunguzare moved towards the lions, who were devouring the meat. The lions left their kill and retreated a little. With her daughter on her back, her mother stood there shocked as one of the lions approached their kill, tore off a big chunk of meat, and hurled it at Zunguzare. She simply clapped her hand in reverence and thanked the lions for the food. They took the meat to a homestead of the local people and told them that lions had killed an animal. The following morning, the locals found the carcass abandoned by the lions.

My mother was a woman of integrity. Having lost her husband in 1971, she braved on for the next 34 years, leading a family of children, grandchildren and great grandchildren. She was blessed with eight children, four boys and four girls. Unfortunately, my brother died young, so she was left with seven of us. Along the way, my father had married two other wives, who had eight children between them. My mother was his first wife and oldest of them all.

She saw it all: the good, the bad and the ugly during her life in the Kawanzaruwa family. She even braved the arrival of the final wife, her own niece: who her husband forcefully took to make his wife after an agreement with her brother. My father paid lobola (dowry) in full for my mother; the in-laws were so happy they promised him another wife. Again, this was customary during that era. Wives or women were a commodity to be abused, which went unchallenged by anyone.

That my father had the right to obtain his new wife against my mother's wishes generated considerable bad blood between the two of them for a long period, until my mother finally gave in. By now, the new wife was pregnant with her first child. The dowry used to marry her was from my sister's husband, who had helped my family with some herds of cattle. My father had taken payment straight to my mother's family to pay for her niece, creating another cycle of promises. This niece had to bear a child who would be given to the son-in-law, who was already married to two of my sisters.

Unfortunately, the pregnancy brought a son. My brother-in-law was furious, but this was God's wish. He was so angry that he threatened my father and wanted all his cattle back. By now my ailing father had no energy to fight back, as his health was failing him. He gave in to the ensuing arguments and left everything to fate. In 1970, my sister was born: that she was a girl broke the animosity between my family and that of my sister's husband.

My father was well known in Chawanda, our village, as a good man who distributed land - his own land - to people who came to settle in the area. He was a kind man who sympathised with everyone in need. He had come to settle here following advice from our uncle: possessed by a spirit medium (Mhondoro), he warned him not to raise his family where he then was in Chesa, across the River Ruya.

There was a cultural belief that a clan could not stay in the same area where the spirit lived, for fear of death. There is a story that five of my father's cousins had died because of this. They had gone hunting and were mauled by a lion. They never came home. This is why the spirit had advised my father to go further afield. The journey did not start in Chesa. My father's brother had moved the family from Madziva, where it would have held the chieftainship when my father was working in Bindura. This was done without my father's approval.

My mother was a young woman back then; but settling near her own family was not the best thing, as we later discovered. It created some rifts between our family and hers. This was because my mother had requested their inheritance from the stepfather, who had taken all her father's cattle forcefully. There were just three girls in their family; the boys are said to have died young and according to tradition, did not have any say in how the inheritance was distributed. My grandmother had been married to her husband's brother after her own husband had passed on. My grandfather was very rich according to the standards of the time. He owned many cattle herds: which is why his brother took over his wife and the accompanying wealth.

My grandmother was betrothed to the brother; and had children who were later put under my mother's care when all the wealth was lost by the latter's stepfather. Apparently, my mother's uncle and stepfather brought the children to our home and said, 'Here, this is your father's wealth. Look after them'. This was during a year of famine. They grew up in our home, becoming very close to us. However, this also gave an opportunity to my father to see the girls grow and choose one who caught his eye.

My mother was a strong character. We, her children, feared her greatly. My father was very vocal but in her quiet way, my mother made us fear her more than him. She had this mannerism whereby, if she told us something, she would not repeat it - because when she did, a beating would follow from whatever was close to her. One day, I offended her by not moving far away from the cooking area while my sisters were cooking. I had caught a bird on one of my hunting trips and wanted to roast it for supper. She warned me many times to move away and give the girls space. I did not take heed of these warnings and continued with my task. The bird had to be nicely roasted: so when everyone else was having their meal without meat, I would enjoy it. There was no way I would leave it to burn.

I don't know where it came from - but suddenly, I had a metal bowl around my neck, and my head was reeling. She had taken a bowl full of water and bashed it on my head. It was so painful, I forgot all about the delicacy I was roasting. When she realised what she had done, she was in a state of panic, recognising the gravity of her actions. She could not remove the bowl from around my neck, as the base was very small. My parents had to find a saw to cut it off. That was my mother: feeling guilty in the end when she had harmed any of her children. She had so much love for us; she had taken solace in loving and caring for her children after my father had married two other women, leaving their own love to die.

Before I started school, it was my responsibility to accompany her into the bushes to look for berries and anything edible. My mother was resourceful; the skills she taught me became very handy later in life. I coil-trapped birds and collected mushrooms. She taught me to recognise edible mushrooms, as it was very dangerous to just pick any. Most mushrooms are poisonous, though they look bright and inviting. The rule was that if flies did not land on the mushroom, it was probably poisonous. We would go into the densely populated forests to look for natural foods, each time coming across things which our ancestors had also eaten. This could take the form of roots, fruit or anything which could help the family survive. On certain occasions, we hunted for rodents by digging deep into their burrows. This was my favourite pastime and took priority over school. That is why my schooling was affected. I had to join school when I was older, though.

My mother, indeed, was the reason I started school late. Even though my older brother encouraged me hugely to go to school, my mother always defended me. She asked him to leave me alone. He had to force me to leave home, so I could grow up: away from this somewhat sheltered environment.

While I was at Mazowe Secondary School, I heard about my father's illness. He had been diagnosed with prostate cancer. There was no medical treatment back then; he was taken to different witch doctors in the assumption he would be cured. What I found most painful of all was that I was never told when he finally succumbed. My family claim they had to hide it to protect me; as when he passed away in August 1971, I was in the middle of exams. I still have nightmares about the whole experience. How could someone not bid farewell to their own father? I would have given him a fitting farewell. I was deprived of this right and have never forgiven whoever made such a decision.

My father died aged 70. He had accumulated a host of children: 21 in total from the combined efforts of three wives, including my mother. My mother always encouraged us to love one another even if we came from different mothers. Yet the second wife had her own teaching, which caused many rifts between the children. My father had also designed a plan to ensure children enjoyed lifelong relationships. He paired us all up. I was paired with a sister from the other wife whose dowry would become mine to use to marry my own wife. This was customary and brought unity to families; but my father's second wife would not have this. She said she had enough daughters and sons to pair against each other - and would not have another wife's children benefiting from her children.

However, this decision worked against her in the end, as all my sisters got married to well-established husbands who paid their dowry accordingly. Her children, by contrast, were dealt a terrible blow. Two of the boys and their sister died of AIDS: which also claimed their wives, leaving their children as orphans for us to look after. Perhaps this was fate; but perhaps it also had something with the wrong teaching from their mother during their formative years.

One of my half-brothers was so mean, he could not share anything with others. My father predicted he would not be successful in life due to this. He would not help his own brother with school fees, later paid by my brother. This meanness is also evident in his son; it amounts to a generational curse. My father's second wife's entire family did not strive for an education and ended up accusing our father of only concentrating on his first family.

This was a dreadful period full of conflict; even, of violence. According to one story, due to one particular fight between the two of them, my father lost his earlobe after his wife bit a huge chunk out of it! This, it is claimed, led to the illness which later claimed his life. How true this is, is anyone's guess.

After my father's death, life became gloomy for the young families. My two brothers and three sisters were well established and had children of their own. I was the only one left who needed support with school fees. My brother briefly took over when I was in Form Two, but later failed to sustain my education. This led to my needing to seek help from my school; and remaining behind during school holidays to work for my fees.

When I finally got married, my older brother took on the responsibility of a father and helped me through the marriage rites. According to custom, he was supposed to add to what I had gathered but instead, when I took my savings to him to keep for some time, he took a lump sum from my own money for personal use: much to my disappointment and my mother's frustration.

When my wife finally came, she was asked to stay with my brother's family as a daughter-in-law, but I challenged this as my mother was still alive. The decision was based on my mother living in a poor, makeshift kitchen made of mud, erected soon after the war of liberation. When the war intensified between the liberation fighters and Rhodesian forces, people gathered in camps all around the country. These camps had strict rules; anyone found violating them was shot dead on the spot. The other idea was to stop the connection between the people (povo) and the freedom fighters: isolating the latter, who relied on the populace for food and information. To the dismay of the Rhodesian army, the povo continued to serve the fighters in hugely creative ways. For example, women who normally went out to fetch water from the wells hid food items anywhere on their bodies.

My mother was a survivor of this terrible war. She was also known to be stubborn even in old age. The camp keepers were afraid of her because when she got angry, she would sing non-stop for up to 24 hours; this scared the soldiers. At one time, she discovered that her daughter-in-law, my second brother's wife, was having an affair with one of the soldiers in the camp. She went and sat by the security gate and started singing without fear of the guns pointing everywhere. My brother was in Harare at that time, looking for employment. They had to warn him not to return home: if he did, he would be killed. That is how bad the situation was in our village.

So when my wife finally came, she refused to live with my brother's family and joined my mother in the makeshift kitchen. This shocked a lot of people in the community: who thought that my wife, an educated woman, would want to live in better conditions. Her argument was she was the wife of the youngest son, so it was her responsibility to look after her ageing mother-in-law. This led to a series of events which resulted in us building a state-of-the-art kitchen for my mother, who became the envy of the community. She now had a daughter-in-law who was working and could provide for her needs. She used to come and visit us in Harare; and would stay for some time before going back home. This was her life now.

My mother was also a village healer, well known for healing different ailments which hospitals could not. She could heal cataracts with a special herb. She would pound this herb and extract the juice, which she put in a teaspoon to apply to the eye. After a few minutes, the cataracts all came out! She helped a lot of people get their sight back without asking for payment. She taught us how to pass this on to the next generation. Much as she would have loved to continue, she couldn't: especially after I left home for school and finally work, settling in Harare. Yet even now, some of my family members can still use the medication to remove cataracts from an affected eye.

One of the skills she left me was how to trap rodents. Mice are a delicacy in Shona society. We used to dig for mice; sometimes getting over 50 in their den. The mice were a problem at times and hugely destructive to crops. Trapping them helped reduce their numbers and save the crops.

11

Each season brought its own food items from the environment. It used to rain regularly, in contrast to the periodic droughts of recent times. During drought years in 1972 and 1982, people relied on my family for food. The former drought claimed many lives; the latter was even worse, and my wife and I came to the rescue: not only of my immediate family, but part of the village too. We bought many pockets of maize meal and sent them to the village for distribution. Some people had gone hungry for weeks and were almost giving up hope when the food arrived. There was an outcry of appreciation for us from all corners of the village.

This support and help were repeated in 2012, when another drought struck Mount Darwin and the surrounding provinces. It had not rained at all that year; people who survived on subsistence farming found it very difficult to cope. We were in the UK - but when we heard the pleas from our own families in Zvimba and Mount Darwin, we had to act. We sent money, so bags of mealie meal could be bought. The bags were distributed to our immediate families, but what we later heard was shocking. We were told that the food was a lifeline to many.

When people heard that there was such a big parcel in our village, they came with containers: some of them as small as a teacup, just to have a small amount to make porridge for the family. When we visited Zimbabwe at the end of that year, people came to thank us personally. We did not know the impact of the help we had provided. This was years after my mother had passed away.

The time I bade goodbye to my mother in preparation for my flight to join my wife and daughter in the UK was not a happy one. I didn't know that it would be the last time I would speak to her. When she died, I recalled when she'd said that maybe I would never see her alive again. It was hugely painful, but I've had to accept it. I really miss my mother; growing up, the bond between me and her was very strong. This was, perhaps, because of her educational stories. She always had an explanation for everything. She taught us that a rainbow was a big, beautiful snake; when one appeared, it was looking for its mate. She also told stories about her own life experiences as the first-born child, and the responsibilities she had to shoulder.

My mother's strength kept the family together after my father's death. She survived him for another 34 years. She was a pillar to the whole extended family; the other two wives had left the home to her and got married elsewhere. She had survived the war, numerous droughts and many more life-threatening situations. I admired my mother so much that I named my daughter (her second name) after her. Her friends had coined her 'Kurifidha' (feeding oneself): not only was she a good cook, but she enjoyed feeding herself as well.

I heard the news of her passing on 5 November 2005; my life has never been the same since. I could not believe it, and even lost the will to cry. I was just numb. I would have loved so much to have attended her funeral, but the political situation would not permit it. I had to hold on to the pain I felt, even aged 50. We were told that her funeral was memorable, as we managed to send money for her burial. She was a good woman, who endured a great deal to keep her family intact.

When, later, I travelled to Zimbabwe to see where she was buried, it took a while for me to believe she was really gone from my and our family's lives. It was very difficult. The experience left me having dreams of her on numerous occasions. I dreamt of her sitting with all of us in the round kitchen, where she told stories as she prepared food for us. It was so vivid, I had to tell my wife about these dreams.

Rest in Peace, Maria Chahwa.


*Ode to Maria, the Merry Matriarch*
Maria, Oh Maria the merry matriarch,
Mother, grandmother of a blossoming people,
Chahwa, the proud She-Elephant our royal,
To her husband and family, she was loyal,
The girl who ran away from death guarded by lions
In the untrodden forest paths on her mother's back,
Even the river showered her with fish, she knew no lack;
Kurifidha, the one who feeds herself, how resourceful,
In the famine she fed her brood on wild leaves and tubers,
A woman of integrity, fearless in the face of adversity
And with a heart of gold, she harboured no animosity,

How she sat all day at a military post singing defiant songs;
The songs of freedom that still echo in all our hearts,
Wise among many, how she imparted wisdom
Into the little hearts of her children and grandchildren
With interesting stories and acts of kindness,
On Maria, Oh Maria, you may be long dead
Yet your life still flows in our veins and love in our hearts.

## My sister, Phoebe

My sister, Nyepudzai (now Phoebe), was born very intelligent: the most talented girl among my four sisters. Two of them, Ennia and Esima, have since died. I have picked Phoebe out of all of them because of her unique traits which made her stand out from the crowd. Phoebe went to school on her own initiative, igniting a period of friction in the family as my father was against the idea of educating a girl. When the family migrated to our present home, schools were few and far between in that area. Upon settling there, my sister was given the task of looking after my maternal grandfather's cattle. As my father was not very convinced about educating girls, this was his excuse for not sending Phoebe to school.

Phoebe desperately wanted to go to school. Her sibling, my older brother who was younger than her, was being educated. This did not go down well with her; so one day, she approached the then headteacher and asked him to allow her into his school. The head demanded fees; and as Phoebe was eager for this opportunity, she brought one of her chickens and was allowed into school. She spent three years there, but due to lack of parental support, especially from our father, left after Standard Three. At this level, she was equipped with the vital skills of reading and writing. After this short stint in education, she was forced to stay at home with all my other sisters until old enough to get married.

Traditionally, when it came to marriage, my clan usually recommended certain families. The predominant custom in the family was similar to betrothal. The eldest sister in the family had fallen victim to this. She was betrothed to a man who had danced so well at a family ceremony, this pleased my father and other male members of the family so much that it warranted gifting him a wife. The man in question was possessed with an ancestral spirit. He was given to my other sister, who was only five years old. Upon realizing that a five-year-old cannot possibly be wife material, she was replaced by my other sister: who was mature enough. This was how my eldest sister obtained her husband. They were married for over 50 years until he died of mental illness.

Phoebe, though, was third in line of my four sisters, always clashed with our father; and when it came to her getting married, there were problems. She attempted suicide once and tried to run away from home. An already married older man proposed to her to become his second wife. She resisted this proposal for months until she could not stand it anymore. She took a rope and tried to hang herself. According to her, she survived because the rope was not strong enough - so it snapped, and she fell onto the floor. She did not give up. That night, she collected her belongings and walked out. She says that as she passed our grandmother's grave, she heard a sharp voice laughing, asking her why she was running away from home. The voice said, 'Are you the first one to face this? Go back and get married'.

So, she returned and married the man she had resisted for such a long period. Her life with him yielded positive results. My sister became the pillar and saviour of her own and our family. Her husband ended up marrying two other girls from our family because of his admiration of Phoebe's extraordinary traits. The fourth wife came from another extended Kawanzaruwa family. All four were close relatives. The family became one of inter-related children.

In terms of her influence on who I became, Phoebe was instrumental in many ways. Having been married to Josaya Tsikai Chidavaenzi, a prominent businessman who later became a political detainee, she was financially powerful and able to support us as a family. I became one of the beneficiaries. My failure at my first attempt at Standard Six resulted in my older brother deciding to make me leave home, as my mother's influence on my education was becoming too much. Being the last born at the time, I was spoiled. She did not want me to go to school; and instead preferred that I accompany her to hunt for rodents.

My formative years in school were the most trying ones; I found every opportunity to run away. My dislike of school was made worse when, one day, girls laughed at my torn short trousers. I had to walk backwards, as they could see everything possible through the holes. This was not the only embarrassment. I also used to wear my sisters' blouses as shirts to school. This made me a laughing stock many a time, reducing my love for education. I therefore enjoyed going on mini-hunting trips with my mother, but my schoolwork suffered.

Later, I was 'shipped off' to my sister, Ennia, so her husband could send me to school on payment of the balance of lobola. I experienced many hardships after they also sent me to live with my brother-in-law's sister and her family. Her existence depended on working on a white man's farm called Dick Hark, near Mount Darwin. I had to work for my food and education, sometimes stealing maize cobs from the farm to be served as food. Yet on certain days, I had to be content with leftovers from her own children after they were full. I watched them eat and when they were done, fed on the remnants.

This was cruelty at its worst. The lady was heartless and did not hide her hatred of me. It was clear she'd been forced to have me under her roof. The farm workers relied on rations, so an extra mouth was a burden. At the end of the second week, I was told that the maize crop in the farm was getting ripe and edible; so, one evening, I was given a sack and told to go into the nearest plot. This was close to our huts. I did it tactfully and brought back about 20 cobs. The family was happy; from that week on, I was given full meals.

During the third week, I was sent to the field again: whereupon I had a near-death experience! This time, word had been spread that the guards would be out to flush out hogs, which were a problem in the farm. They fed on the crop. As I plucked the last cob, I heard some sounds followed by gunshots. The bullet missed me by a whisker. I dropped down and lay flat on the ground: my heart pounding hard. I lay there for a good two hours.

It was almost midnight when I found a safe way home. I told the lady what had happened. This had to stop - so it did. This did not please my cousins, so they provided me with the bus fare to go back home. I left feeling like an abused loser. I had not got what I had gone there for. However, I had learnt a valuable lesson: never be persuaded to steal by someone else.

This was when Phoebe began to enter the picture. Even after my return home, my older brother remained adamant that I should not stay with the family if I wanted an education. So I tried again at a school in Chisecha, near the border with Mozambique, where we had to bring everything for our own upkeep. We had to build our own pole and dagga huts to sleep in while attending school. My initial plan in moving to Chisecha was to stay with Phoebe, whose husband had a shop near the school. When I got there, they had moved to another place, so I had to content myself with the Katsapo Boarding School, as it was popularly known. The name was derived from the need to bring everything to make a home there in a pillow-like sack (katsapo). I stayed there for only one term with two other boys, Kidson and Patson. Later, I gave these names to my half-brothers to replace theirs.

When I left, I went to Kamutsenzere Primary School: where the head took me in together with his two brothers to complete my Standard Six. Phoebe and her husband paid for my education. I became very attached to the head, Mr Chipatura, who trusted me more than his brothers. He trained me in many skills which later helped me. During holidays, I used to stay with my sister at their shop in Kamutsenzere. They looked after my wellbeing until I completed school. Their home became my second home. My sister was blessed with sons and a daughter: the first-born being Morris Tichafa. I became his godfather.

## My wife, Gallie

I want to include my wife, Gallie, in my own story because she has contributed immensely to what we have become as a family. One day, I was speaking to my mother-in-law, who revealed how she'd borne her only child: now my wife. My mother-in-law was the first born in her family. Her father ended up with three wives, just like my father. Her only child was the result of being forced into a polygamous marriage. Her aunt asked for her to become her husband's second wife, to prevent her husband from marrying outside the family. At the time, my late father-in-law intended to marry a wife from the Ndebele tribe: considered a taboo, as many believed this tribe would take over the family.

The option of marrying within someone's own clan, preferably the brother's daughter, was practiced a lot in Zimbabwe, where it was possible even for a woman to hunt for a second wife for her husband. This was done to prevent the husband from getting a wife unrelated to her. It worked well in some polygamous settings. A Shona saying states that however beautiful a polygamous setting is, it's like a nest full of thorns, as it was in my mother-in-law's case. It created problems, so my wife was born into a troubled situation.

My mother-in-law was frogmarched to her husband by her father. The husband was a policeman who lived in a police camp, so was well off financially; the British South Africa Police (BSAP), the colonial police force, was considered the best-paying employer by many. The same aunt who had initiated the marriage soon changed her mind as my mother-in-law was receiving favours from her husband. Young, beautiful and well educated, she was subsequently mistreated, verbally and physically abused by her aunt.

My wife's survival was at stake right from birth. Her mother was denied food and later kicked out of her husband's home. During that era, going to hospital was very difficult due to distance, cost and lack of knowledge. Babies survived by the grace of God, as immunisation had yet to be introduced. My wife and I were born in these similar circumstances, as were most if not all those born during this period. My wife grew up at her maternal grandparents' home.

As a young baby, she almost died. She fell ill from measles; and as she fell into a coma, many people thought she had passed away. On arrival at the clinic, the doctor resuscitated her by wrapping her in a hot towel, and she started breathing. In the years that followed, my wife grew up through various ups and downs. She later joined her mother in her second marriage in Zvimba (Mashonaland West), another part of

Zimbabwe. Her story was one of colossal struggle for survival and education.

My wife was raised by her mother in a moderately poor family, along with five stepsiblings from her stepfather's former wife. Following the failure of their arranged marriage, her mother divorced her father when she was just a few months old. A qualified teacher, her mother had to leave home to look for employment, in order to raise her and send her to school. She was left with her grandparents until age five. This experience led her to acquire certain skills such as cooking, and the ability to look after family members from a very early age. Indeed, two of her aunts contracted polio, so were rendered unable to perform most house chores. Aged just five, this resulted in her being charged with looking after them.

Subsequently, her mother met and married her stepfather: who raised her, together with his own five children from a previous marriage. Following this, Gallie joined her mother, who had now established a new home and family in Zvimba. This was where she started her schooling. Without going into much detail about her early school life, I can certainly relate that it was not a pleasant experience according to the stories she has told. At times, indeed, she was unable to attend school because her mother could not raise her school fees. Her stepdad, a mean man, did not see the value of education. He was a proud man who considered himself a successful, self-made driver; but he had no interest in educating anyone, let alone a stepchild.

They depended very much on subsistence farming. Each summer, they were required to prepare the land for tilling, planting crops and harvesting them for their own consumption as well as commercial purposes, like any other farming family in Zimbabwe. If the crops did not do well in any given year, the family would struggle for food as well as school fees. They also did a great deal of gardening of various types of vegetables, which they would then sell.

Her childhood experiences and upbringing had an enormous impact on the striver she became, both as a wife and professional woman. In effect, they provided training in skills which would prove vitally important: problem-solving, resilience and perseverance, among many others.

My mother-in-law values education, so did all she could to protect her daughter. My wife was sent to boarding school, back when it was a real struggle to send a daughter to such institutions. Through huge determination, my wife made it to the top in education. She sailed through primary school and on to higher education, even though the environment she did it in was not at all friendly.

I did not know Gallie until she was introduced to me as our tenant by my friend, Jerome Piroro, who had taught her at the boarding school. Soon after Zimbabwean independence in 1980, my friend and I teamed up to buy a house in one of the more affluent suburbs of Harare. Gallie was doing her 'O' Levels at the time. She came to our house looking for accommodation as a former primary school student of my friend. We gave her a room to stay. At that time, I was not staying in Harare. I was teaching at Henderson Research Primary School, some 50 kilometres out of Harare, in the Mazowe area. I came during the weekends. As a teacher, I was very strict with students, and viewed Gallie as one too.

As time went by, something happened between me and Gallie. We fell for each other. With a difference of over ten years, I had to be careful, but love knows no bounds. Gallie developed a dangerous liking for me, and I became very much attracted to her. We became very strong friends; I did all I could to keep us together. She continued with school while I did the same with my teaching job.

Our love grew to great heights, which began to affect Gallie's education. As a very able student, she sought to forge ahead with her studies, but concentration became difficult: so much so that by the end of her four-year secondary school education, she was finding it increasingly challenging to study while focusing on our newly found love. She could not make it to the required five 'O' levels. She had fallen pregnant as a student with our baby, Mavreen Tariro. As head girl of the school, she had disappointed her teachers, mother and herself.

Our marriage was arranged promptly to 'hide' the pregnancy. Before deciding to marry, we had foolishly decided to terminate it. Fear mixed with ignorance almost made us lose our valued first daughter, Tariro.

The Lord prevented it. We performed our traditional marriage ceremony and were declared husband and wife. During this process, I left the house I'd bought with my friend, Jerome, and Gallie and I bought our own home: where we continued to live as husband and wife. We fell in love in 1981 and were married in December 1982. Our first daughter was born in March of the following year. We were later blessed with two more children, Tawanda Malvern and Takudzwa Marilyn.

Usually in Zimbabwe, a woman's education is disturbed either by early marriage or familial beliefs. Most do not bother to seek self-improvement soon after marriage. This is gradually changing; and in Gallie's case, I encouraged her to read, which really connected with her. She surprised us all and her friends when she embarked on a reading spree. I bought her numerous novels and helped her register for evening classes. In no time, she had obtained all the required GCE and Advanced Level subjects.

She did not stop there. She secured a place to teach secondary English and Home Economics in Chiweshe, Mashonaland Central province: which was where her love for teaching was ignited. At the end of that year, 1987, she joined Belvedere Teachers College to train as a teacher in these subjects; after three years, she obtained a teaching certificate. That made it two teachers in the family. She could now teach in secondary school while I remained a primary school teacher. As time passed, she encouraged me to improve my status as well: because opportunities were appearing for teachers to improve themselves financially and professionally. I gained a Diploma in teaching, which improved my profile at work and led to my appointment as Deputy Headmaster. My wife went further: studying for a degree part-time, while being a teacher and mother to, by now, three children.

She completed her Bachelor's degree in Educational Administration, Planning and Policy Studies with the University of Zimbabwe. I trailed behind her as I studied for a degree in Counselling with the same university. I did not complete the studies; instead, I followed Gallie to the UK, where I embarked on further postgraduate study. All this was done through my wife's encouragement and support. I now truly appreciated how loving and caring she was. We became a strong family team: supporting and encouraging ourselves to improve. Our status in society changed to one of respect; our children followed us as their role models. They all have degrees now and are very well qualified in their jobs.

During Gallie's childhood, she struggled for everything, including school fees. At one point, she walked to her boarding school with her mother about 50 kilometres away, to plead with the Head to allow her to sit for the final Grade 7 exams the following morning. She arrived at the school at eight in the morning; the exam had already started. Quickly, the Head rushed her into the exam room, thinking she would pay the fees later: only to discover she could not. Out of sympathy, he allowed her to complete all the exams, but then agreed that she would not collect her certificate.

This same scenario occurred when she wanted to pay for her 'O' Level exam fees. It was just $11, but she could not afford it. When she studied for her Bachelor's, we were not in good financial standing as a family: this proved another struggle for Gallie. She had not paid her fees in full - which resulted in her attending graduation but not obtaining her certificate. I had to collect it on her behalf later, when she had already left for England to study for her Master's. It is such a pity that someone must suffer so much when there are people around who can help.

In Gallie's case, she had two highly educated, well-to-do uncles. One of them, who has since passed away, stopped helping her because he was not getting along with her mother. The other, who later became a minister in the Zimbabwean government, decided to follow his wife's decision to help send her own brothers and sisters to school. This disadvantaged Gallie, who was moved out of their house as there was not enough space. This was when she came to look for accommodation at our place: the start of our future together.

Gallie would go on to accomplish a huge amount. After completing her teacher training, she started working at Cranborne Boy's High School, a short distance from our home in Hatfield. This was the beginning of her career. Initially, she marked 'O' level English Language.

This became our second income: Gallie was invited to mark in centralised places across the country and would return with a lot of money. This sustained us in many ways, even paying for our children's boarding fees.

At Cranborne, Gallie researched the prospects of going abroad for further studies. One day, she had taken her class to the library for a reading session when she came across a catalogue from a university in the UK offering scholarships. She was naturally interested; one thing led to another, and she received a firm offer from the same university. Gallie had again set the pace for the whole family.

Gallie was not the first person from the school planning on going abroad. A horde of other teachers had already flown out of the country. However, Gallie was the only one who followed the correct channel when applying for study leave and a student visa through the British Embassy. She was granted both - so immediately after graduating from the University of Zimbabwe, flew out on the same day on a journey which would take all of us to the UK.

For me, this was a tough time, as I had a home and kids to look after. It was a stressful period both financially and emotionally. People always imagine that when someone goes abroad, everything is organised in advance; but at the time Gallie moved to the UK, the Zimbabwean economic crisis was underway. It was very difficult to make ends meet, even more so with two children in boarding school. Now a student in north-east England, Gallie could not get a job immediately. It took a few months for her to settle in and find her way into the job market.

By this time, our oldest daughter had joined her in the UK: a huge relief. She'd been bent on joining her mother, as she had just turned 17. This was the best decision we ever made; by the following year, it would have been very difficult to go abroad. Our two other children and I joined them in July 2002, making us one big family once again.

Fortunately, Gallie obtained a well-paid teaching job: a major improvement for our dwindling resources. Yet she wanted to see to it that the family was financially stable. At one point, she had three jobs: teaching during mornings until 3pm; before rushing to Marks and

Spencer's, where her work started at 4pm. Immediately after finishing at 8pm, Gallie took off one uniform and put on another, for a night shift at an old people's home. All this on top of her studies! This was her life for a few months until something permanent came along.

The money from her labour was sent home: boosting our position not only financially, but also in the community, where we'd always been looked down upon as we were teachers. Now I walked with a spring in my step. The kids had money in the bank; and I had a lot stashed away too. Each time I visited the bank, I received preferential treatment when the managers saw my balance.

When Gallie arrived in Sunderland, which would become our permanent home for many years, she immediately looked for our church, the Salvation Army. She found one where she was treated very well. Everyone at the Corps made sure Gallie was comfortable. One of the families, the Loshes, literally adopted her as their own. She used to go to theirs for lunch every Sunday after service. This became a tradition even when the whole family was together. We had a lot of support from this family in cash and kind. The rest of the church used to bring food items and warm clothes. Life became very comfortable for us; a dream come true!

How we started our new life as a family in the UK, though, is a topic for a later chapter.

# CHAPTER 2:

# EDUCATION IN TROUBLED ZIMBABWE

When we were growing up, we were told a great deal about the situation in Zimbabwe. The elders sometimes used pans to avoid being labelled as anti-colonial. One day, I attended a secret political rally, where all the talk was about everybody being a 'son of the soil'. We were asked to get some soil and given a penny each. The leader asked us to choose between the soil and the coin. I could buy a couple of sweets with the coin, so I chose that. All young people chose the coin. We did not know anything about a handful of dirty soil. It was later explained to us that the soil represented our heritage. Money would come from that soil. Suddenly, I understood what this meant.

The story of Zimbabwe is a hugely painful one. Politically, it has been a constant struggle for survival. People took up arms to fight the colonial government. That was not wrong in the eyes of many Zimbabweans. The situation had to be corrected. The war started in north-east Zimbabwe. This was the Second Chimurenga War: following the 1966 one, fought out during a one-time battle in Mashonaland West. When we entered the Second Chimurenga, I was just finishing my 'O' levels. Books I had read about wars explained that they are often controversial, deadly, and do not end well. They resurface and often take on different forms.

In Zimbabwe, the war left people drained: especially in rural areas. Some families were destroyed completely. Sons and daughters went to war with the intention of righting the political situation, never to come back. Those who did return were either maimed or psychologically wounded; some were victims of rape, torture and emotional abuse. Many of those who could not make it lie in unmarked graves. This is what is so painful. This is not politics alone, but a matter of human rights. If things turn out so badly, where do the survivors turn?

Zimbabwe has a fascinating history, having been occupied by various groups: in particular, the Bantu tribes. The main occupants were the San tribes, now known as the Bushmen. The Bushmen were eventually driven away to present day Botswana.

My own tribe, Bantu, is said to have immigrated from the north and crossed the Zambezi River. I belong to the Nhari Unendoro group. This is a totem. The Shona tribe, if not all the Bantu tribes, are grouped into totems. Most totems are based on animals. The Bantu way of life was centred around hunting and gathering. This probably created a system where the early Bantu tribes called their group by animal names. We are identified as 'Unendoro'. The men are called 'Nyamasvisva'; while the women are known as 'Chihoro'. I have discovered that a cow and an elephant, 'Nzou', are the names under which my tribe falls.

Name any animal, and you'll discover it has people who identify totem-wise with it. The major ones are Nzou (Elephant); or 'Soko' (Monkey/Baboon). The Ndebele tribe uses names to identify with the animals. They have names like 'Njovhu', 'Mpofu', 'Nyati', and many others. There are also animal names, such as the elephant and the buffalo.

The totems helped stop the marriage of close relatives. Most Shonas avoid marrying into a family which they share a totem with. Interestingly, men and women from a certain tribe behave in a particular manner. Some are identified by being warlike; while others are peaceable. Nhari Unendoro group men are identified by being very calm, quiet and composed. The women, however, are mostly overbearing, at times arrogant, but very hard-working and accommodating.

The Nharis are identified by two ancestors, Biri and Ganyire. They are said to have led a group to mysteriously cross the Zambezi River as they journeyed from the north, through present day Mozambique.

## The coming of the white man

Family history says that our group was residing in the Shamva-Madziva area when the first white settler came. My great grandfather was asked to pay and surrender to the white man to gain protection. This was colonisation in progress. He was asked to pay a coin; upon receipt, the white man declared him a Chief of this area.

At this stage, most men were being conscripted into hard labour and forced to leave their families. They were forced into road construction. After the Pioneer Column arrived at Fort Salisbury in 1890, teams of explorers, hunters and mineral prospectors were sent into the country.

The white man who first came into the area where my people were living was called Pari. He was brought in a hammock, all the way from Fort Salisbury. His mode of transport was precisely this hammock. Pari was transported in this way from village to village. Once he arrived at one village, it became their turn to ferry him to the next one. He was carried like a baby. By the time he arrived at my ancestor's village, the Head had disappeared into the mountains.

This was when my great grandfather was confronted and asked to pay the ransom. He nearly obtained the chieftainship. He told them there was a tribal chief, but he could not be found. He reported this to the Chief upon his return; he had almost lost his leadership to us. The rule had been that the first person to see and talk to the white man would be made leader of that area. This was the beginning of the white man's influence in present day Zimbabwe.

When the Europeans came to Africa, they believed they were a superior race and that black people were not as intelligent and wise as themselves. Racism was normalised into slavery and servitude. The people were forced out of their land and homes. All the good land was taken forcefully.

Zimbabwe can essentially be divided into three geographical regions: the Low Veld, Middle Veld and High Veld. The whites drove out most of the black people to the Middle and Low Veld, where it is very hot: with some areas extremely dry and inhabitable. The High Veld became white land; all the way from the south, towns began to grow. The High Veld has good rainfall; temperatures are mild and suitable for farming. Areas like Nyanga became the white men's home. Ever since 1890, the issue of land has been enormously painful for my country: leading, ultimately, to a 13-year guerrilla war of independence.

## Self-rule

This situation can be interpreted in various ways politically. Zimbabwe has become divided by the issue of land. Some have lost while others have gained; but the worst thing is those whose sons and daughters died in the war of independence are still suffering. The concept of a political party having its own youth, ex-combatants or ex-detainees divides people into groups. The danger is tribal warfare, culminating in racial and ethnic cleansing and genocide. Perhaps this is why today, Zimbabwe is in a state of denial, with its people traumatised and subject to abuse, neglect and hopelessness. Murder and rape are rife; as are human rights abuses and corruption.

As a visitor, I had the shock of my life when I saw a 'spike': a tool used by the police. It is thrown under a moving car to puncture all the tyres. This tool and the baton can damage a car, leading to high repair costs. The baton is used to smash the windscreen if the motorist misbehaves. This is malicious damage of property. All this has resulted in lawlessness; the law of the jungle rules.

Roads have become killing grounds. These issues, which should be discussed in parliament, are not given priority. Any reasonable person should see the use of spikes and batons as evil and inhuman. Where else in the world are these used? It is abusive and unforgivable.

## Education, the secret of our success

Major changes in my life started in the 1960s, when my quest for another form of education took over. I began to visualise what the books were saying. For example, my brothers talked of the town, which to me only existed in pictures. I envied some of the boys, who used to travel to boarding schools in their magnificent khaki uniform. I had a serious stumbling block. I had failed to make substantial progress in my reading. I was probably dyslexic up to the sixth year of primary school. Some progress occurred when my elder brothers transferred me to another school. I went to that school against my mother's will.

Yet staying at home had, in part, caused my poor school performance; and I needed assistance in school fees from our brother-in-law. So I left home: but my major anguish was leaving my parents, especially my mother. It was decided that I should join my sister. This did not turn out as comfortably as I had anticipated.

At this remote establishment, I had to stay with the headteacher - a friend of my brother-in-law - in his home. I never had direct contact with my sister. The headteacher was a senior bachelor; his family was made up of his brothers and all their extended family. I found my place between them; and as we shared the same totem, became one of them. Quickly, I got used to living with people who were not my immediate family and assumed the role of a housekeeper.

I proved a trusted child in the house: so much so that within a month, I had been entrusted with the keys to the main bedroom. Later, I learnt that the guys used to inspect the bedroom for small change and steal if they could. They tried all the tricks in the book to get the keys from me; but failed.

One day, I was surprised. Another brother, who was my age, was told to trick me so I would release the keys. Unaware of this, I was asked to accompany him to the shop; but we changed course midway, and he led me to a bush. We arrived at a tree stump and he told me to inspect it. I thought it was a game. There on the stump were a few silver coins. I was frightened; money could not come from bushes, and such money was associated with graves. There were fresh graves nearby, so I bolted. He called me back and explained. We took the cash and had a feast of sweets and tasty buns. The story got through to our big brother, who disciplined us; and the stealing ended immediately.

However, my academic performance was still not good at all, so I was pulled two classes back. Repeating brought good results: after another two years, I had reached the top ten in our class. All along, I had been classified as not very intelligent, even by my family. When I tasted success in this small way, I began to see some light at the end of the tunnel. After staying away from home for more than two years, I realised that as a boy, I was becoming more and more stable in my personality. I agree with Giddens (2002) when he suggests that childhood abilities such as handling emotions and getting on well with others are good predictors of an intelligent person. Gardner (1993: 22) agrees: 'Interpersonal intelligence is the ability to understand other people: what motivates them, how they work and how to work co-operatively with them'.

One of the things I learnt was to comfort myself at times of want and crisis. The final two years of my primary education left me drained. There was not much physical and emotional support from home. This became worse when I left the sanctuary of the headteacher, who had helped me so much for those two vital years. For now, I moved to Katarira School: a very remote school, but the only one providing Standard 4 in the Dande area in 1960. This proved a major challenge.

The nearest place I had to make my home was where my sister was - but that was 15km away. I got a bicycle from home; but it was old and kept giving me problems. I was often late for lessons. Finally, the bike could take no more. One day, I forced it onto the road without tyres. I didn't get very far, so had to resort to walking the 15km. One day after lessons, I travelled home to my sister's place. I was late, so after eating wild fruit I fell asleep up in a tree; but had a sense of safety.

In no time, I was asleep. The area was not safe at all, as it was infested with wild animals. There was a lot of howling and shrill noises, but I continued in peaceful sleep. I must have been up the tree for a good three hours when I heard distant voices. At first, I ignored them; but all of a sudden, heard my name being called. My sister had come looking for me. She called and called. I finally responded when I made sure it was her. There were stories of hyenas calling people like they were their next of kin, so I made sure not to prematurely expose myself. I responded when I saw the group. My sister was crying. I had to abandon the idea of travelling to school. The teacher was concerned about my performance as a result of missing some of the morning lessons.

That term ended with me staying at the school, as I teamed up with friends and had an idea. We started a compound known, quite literally, as 'Katsapo Boarding School'. This simply meant a self-constructed home near the school, to ease our travel problems. We brought our own food and bedding. My elder brother took over: but he never came back to the school after he had brought me food. For a year, I had to rely on scavenging. I resorted to my skills as a herd boy. I trapped birds, collected local fruit and shared what I could in exchange for a meal.

I survived on what nature could provide and gave thanks to the Dande environment for meeting my needs. Wild fruit, locusts and small birds were easy to find. Life went on; and with my friends, we enjoyed our lessons. Even washing clothes and bathing were luxuries I could not afford at times. Not only that; but in an area plagued by malaria, the nearest clinic was a whole day's journey away on foot. Fortunately, I never contracted any serious bouts.

By the end of the year, it was clear that I could not continue living in the Dande area. My sister had left to start a new business in our home area. This was a blow, as now I had nobody to support or look after me. Naturally, my academic performance had been seriously affected. I was called home and enrolled at our home school on condition that I looked after the headteacher's cattle in exchange for school fees. I did it for a term, before leaving for another venture. One of my brothers-in-law was asked to provide my fees. He was supposed to provide lobola which I could convert into fees. He had no money, so sent me to his sister: whose husband was a labourer at one of the farms in Bindura, Matepatepa.

Chivhere Farm School was a unique kind of school, where the farmer provided a basic education to disadvantaged children. We supplied our labour; the farmer provided education. The so-called teachers operated the school on shifts. One group worked in the field in the morning and attended lessons in the afternoon, and vice versa. I dreaded working in the fields but enjoyed herding the farmer's cattle. This was less tiring and gave me the chance to read when the cattle had grazed enough and were calm.

In terms of learning, I accrued very little, because our teachers were untrained. They had nothing to offer in terms of teaching experience; consequently, their methods of lesson delivery were crude. However, this was still better than not going to school at all. This experience was faced by many in what was then still colonial Rhodesia. Most people had to struggle for their education. The colonial state had two separate education systems: one for privileged, white minority groups; the other for the predominant blacks. During that era, going further with education was a nightmare. For example, only 12.5% of black children leaving primary school in 1968 were allowed to proceed to secondary school. The rest became redundant, and usually found employment in the industrial or farming sectors.

In today's world, the farm where I and so many other children studied would be considered as overseeing child labour; tantamount even to abuse. Children went there as boarders, with accommodation provided by the farmer. The students brought food and blankets. They would stay there for the full term without going back home, working on the farms before and after classes for the fees.

Those who attended such schools report that it was not at all pleasant. They might have gained skills of self-reliance but qualifications wise, there was nothing worthwhile apart from writing and reading. I could say the same of my own experience, except I managed to find the motivation to continue with my studies after leaving the farm school.

After returning home and missing a term, I met a teacher working at Labella Farm School. I went with him, and from that point onwards, never again endured interrupted schooling, apart from having to repeat grades. My experience there was rewarding. There was real learning. However, I struggled with farm work, which was tiring and hard. We worked in shifts. Some classes had morning lessons while others were in the fields. At lunch, we met, ate, and those who had been out in the fields would have afternoon lessons. We exchanged this timetable weekly; but it was difficult to concentrate on afternoon lessons after such hard work, so I often slept during class.

This was noticed by the teacher, who advised I be given other duties. I worked with those who looked after the farm animals. This was the best thing that happened to me on the farm. I could milk the cows and enjoy the grazing lands around the farm. This was less tiring. I began to enjoy the lessons. I still have happy memories of Labella Farm. It was the best place for me to be at that time.

My situation changed when once again, my brother decided to take me to our village school. Even at this point, I could not put on the kind of clothing worn by boys who came home from distant secondary schools: khaki shorts and jumpers. I had never had a decent pair of shoes; the mere thought of one drove me crazy. This helped motivate me and drive me. I devoted my time to reading. I worked very hard and took a final primary school examination: the Standard Six. I had been promised secondary education if I passed at the end of the year.

These skills helped me when I started my first job: temporary teaching after passing my 'O' levels. This is when I entered another frightening phase of my life. I taught at a school in a remote part of the country. It was a time of war, with the Rhodesian government fighting against the black people in the country. It was a fierce guerrilla conflict which almost claimed my life.

As a teacher, I was supposed to be apolitical, but I took the side of the freedom fighters who would often visit my rural school for supplies. The short period in which I engaged left me politically conscious. I almost left for training as a guerrilla in Mozambique or Tanzania; but an old friend changed my mind and helped me enrol for teacher training.

Training to be a teacher was interesting and rewarding. My three-year course earned me a teaching certificate. Equipped with this, I took up my post as a fully qualified primary school teacher. Having come this far, I began to relax and develop a sense of accomplishment. For seven years, I remained like this until I realised that there was still something for me to do. The challenge came from some of my college friends, who were in managerial positions or heads of schools.

This coincided with the country just gaining its independence, and there was a call for people to go back to school. I grabbed this chance; but encountered problems in balancing my social life. I was thinking of marrying and raising a family. I got married and found new priorities and obligations. Yet I worked very hard for my wife and children to go on with their education.

## Education and politics in Zimbabwe

Zimbabweans hunger for education. Historically, the provision of education was not in the state's hands, but the preserve of a few. Missionaries provided basic education, but only to their own converts. Most of the learning was based on the three Rs: emphasizing Bible reading. Zimbabwe was dominated by Church mission schools; most Zimbabweans became Christian as a result. State education came at a later stage: a two-tier system for Europeans and Africans. This was an apartheid system which called for separate development. The Africans were supposed to be used as tools to develop the progress of the white men. In South Africa, where the apartheid system was legalised, an African was meant to be a slave and only fit to be a woodcutter. The atrocities perpetrated by the whites against the blacks provoked anger, retaliation and mistrust across southern Africa. Only recently, a white man and his colleagues were filmed trying to force a black worker on a farm into a coffin.

Education for black people was bottlenecked, so only a few would make it into secondary school. I suffered from this when awarded Grade 3 in my first attempt at Standard Six. With only 20% allowed to move on, I had to repeat the year to improve my grade. Essentially, I had passed - but most blacks were not afforded the opportunity to gain a secondary education, lest they became educated enough to speak the language effectively. Even those who were educated to degree level were not allowed to speak the coloniser's language, meaning correct English. They were only allowed to speak broken English (Chiraparapa), which would always make them feel submissive to the 'master'. I grew up in this regime; yet was determined to pursue an education as a means of removing myself from the chains of poverty and improving the status of my family.

So much so that I decided to repeat the year under a new name, Blessing, with a new birth certificate to boot. I had to cheat the bottleneck in order to progress. I re-enrolled; and this time, I passed. That was in 1968. It had taken me two years to pass through Standard Six. Now I had the springboard into secondary education which I had so desperately desired.

In the Federation of Rhodesia and Nyasaland, and under governments such as Ian Douglas Smith's, life for the black man was enormously challenging. I remember being kicked and pushed out of the way by a white boy as I walked down First Street in Salisbury. I was so embarrassed, because I was being accompanied by girlfriends. This was on the opening day of the school term when we were waiting to be bused to our respective schools. We had wandered into First Street in front of the railway station, where we usually met with the girls who were traveling to Bulawayo.

## Life at Mazowe

Soon after finishing my Standard Six, I enrolled at Mazowe Secondary School, a boys only boarding school in Mazowe-Mashonaland Central. I started there in 1969. The challenge now was securing the school fees required, as my benefactor (my sister's husband, Chidavaenzi), had been imprisoned for political reasons in Hwahwa: along with others such as Robert Mugabe, the future Prime Minister and President.

I found myself in a terrible predicament and had to ask my older brother for help. He was working at a baker's as a delivery man, and not getting enough to spare my fees. He suggested I work in his fields to help his pregnant wife. I did this with a friend who also wanted fees. We worked so hard, I had bruises all over the palms of my hands. In the end, he paid only my friend and said he would pay for my fees later. This was a real blow.

However, his wife came to my rescue, when she suggested I get at least a fraction of the fees needed for the boarding school. My father had to sell a bull to raise more of the money, as he was not well himself to work and help. This little money did not discourage me. To my surprise, when I arrived at the school, not only I had difficulties paying for tuition and boarding fees; many of us were in the same boat. This was a huge relief.

My life at Mazowe, which belonged to the Salvation Army, was of real struggle, especially early on. To survive, I had to be creative. Mending other students' shoes became my livelihood. I only had to worry about school fees, as pocket money was now available to keep until the following term. As for uniforms, my peasant background meant I could not compete with some of the boys in attire and entertainment - I did not have the means to do so - but God was on my side.

I used to pick uniforms from bins; those thrown away by students from rich families, who would not want to start a new term with old ones. I shared these with others in the same predicament because I found more than enough. The money I received from the shoe repairs, as well as small jobs like washing and ironing, supported my upkeep. I even had a surplus to take home to my mother.

At the beginning of each term, I had enough provisions in the form of peanut butter and other odd foods. I could not afford tinned foods, which the boys from town bought. At times I exchanged my own village foods for tinned beans or bread and butter.

Now, God intervened again. During one of those school holidays, one of the missionary teachers (most teachers were foreigners from the Salvation Army) came and asked for my photograph. He said he had found a donor from Australia, who was willing to pay my fees after hearing of my determination. From Form Three until my 'O' Levels, my fees were paid by a third anonymous donor. He became my saviour.

However, I did not stop working in my two 'trades' to raise pocket and upkeep money. Remaining behind while everyone else enjoyed their holiday was now part of my life at Mazowe. I enjoyed this as it gave me financial independence. At home, my family were supportive and happy that I had found the means to get an education. I have always been a loner, so not going home was not a major problem for me.

Most of my friends decided to leave once they reached Form Two, as they were qualified enough to secure employment or even train as a teacher. I braved it out; and am glad I did, because an 'O' Level later became a requirement for many governmental departments, including teacher training colleges. My friend Jerome, though, left school and trained as a teacher at Waddelove Teacher Training College.

## Becoming a teacher

Soon after I completed my secondary education, it was now time for a job search. By this point, I was reasonably well informed about which career path I should follow. I did not accept defeat or failure; but was also blind to competition. I did not compete with anyone nor compare myself unfavourably with others. In my 'O' Levels, I achieved some very good passes in most subjects: except languages, which I had to retake to obtain better grades. I would have liked to move into agriculture or become a health professional. However, I settled on education and trained as a teacher.

I spent the first few months of 1973 at home. I looked for a temporary teaching post and eventually obtained one at Tsengurwe School, after a teacher had been involved in a landmine explosion. I was asked to replace a teacher who was teaching Grade 7, a class preparing for the end of year final examination which could enable them to go on into secondary school. I did a good job. The problem was I was in danger of being dragged into joining the war as a fighter. I had some very close links with the groups of guerrilla fighters who came to the area. Some were keen for me to go with them; but my job was to ensure that my class succeeded at the end of their primary education.

Matters came to a head when the liberation fighters, called the 'comrades' by the local community, came to my school in the middle of the night, seeking food and other provisions. We gave them what we had, and they left peacefully. But subsequently, we were also visited by Rhodesian forces, who aimed to flesh out the guerrillas; and had been alerted by local people known as 'sell-outs'. These people were well known for playing both sides and creating confusion. The fiercest battle involved some of my pupils in a shoot-out; they had been caught in a crossfire. One of the girls had her ear slashed by a bullet.

Another time, I had a huge fright after deciding to visit my family in Chawanda during the evening, on a bike. Just as I was approaching an intersection, there was an enormous bang, which I later realised had happened some kilometres away. I was thrown off the bike and landed about 30m further on. This scared me to death, so I decided not to continue with my trip. These were some of the deadly activities brought about by the war. The comrades were bent on taking back the country and knew no fear.

Chimbambaira, as the landmines were popularly known, were strewn all over the place. They went off anywhere: even at cows, herdsmen and children coming from school. The liberation war left deep scars in most families which are still felt even now. Some lost their sons and daughters who joined the war; others lost them in the villages, where the sell-outs were communicating false information to fighters. My two cousins also left for Chimoio in Mozambique, where they were trained to fight. I never saw them again. I am told that they died in one of the raids in the Mutoko area, when they were returning after the ceasefire process was announced.

I was at Tsengurwe for two terms, teaching some students who were older than me. I was the only breadwinner at the time, and had to provide for the whole family, including my brothers. I would get my salary and give it all to my brother's wife to distribute to the family. My work coincided with famine in Mount Darwin, as the rains had not come. Mount Darwin is well known for farming; but if the rains did not appear, it would be very dry for crops and animals. Thus, my work helped alleviate immediate danger of hunger in my family.

Jerome, now in his final year of teacher training at Waddelove, encouraged me to join him, as they were now focusing on recruiting only those who had gone as far as 'O' Level. This was when it became clear that my decision to complete my secondary education with a GCSE certificate, not only a Junior certificate (JC), had been an excellent one. I applied and was accepted.

In January 1974, I started my teacher training journey: which would take three years to complete. This was just two years after completing Mazowe Secondary School. What a life I experienced there. I did not stop my shoe-making trade, which again helped me beef up my pocket money. I mended shoes at minimal cost; this made me very popular.

My only difficulty was in finding a girlfriend. Women were not interested in me: telling me that I was too gentle, and they wanted 'macho' types. Mostly, I kept myself to myself, and had a few friends in the same situation. Yet I went on to defend the 'macho' boys when they were caught by someone's brother in the local area, looking for girls. I had to defend them and sometimes hid them in my room when others came looking to fight them. This is when I gained some respect among women; but I remained unlucky in love. By then, Jerome had left to teach in a school in Mashonaland West Province, Zvimba.

### The Henderson experience

After I completed Waddelove, I got my first teaching job in Mazowe, at the Henderson Research School. My mother's recommendation had been not to base myself anywhere near home. This was excellent advice: as I later discovered when one of the local boys came to teach at Chawanda School, our local school, after completing his training. He experienced many problems; the community took advantage of him, to the extent of giving away their daughters as would-be wives.

In 1977, when I started at Henderson, I still had very little money or household property. The first thing I bought was a bed, dining table and chairs. My first suit cost $15: an advantage of being very close to Harare, which was a 25-minute journey by bus. Yet Henderson would prove one of the best places I have ever worked at and lived. It provided a sanctuary for bachelors like me. It had all anyone would need. We were provided with food portions to last months, including fresh eggs, milk, beef and chicken.

I joined a small staff, made up entirely of Shonas. Life was cheap even though the salaries were very low. I earned $79.90; not much. I had to supplement my earnings by growing my own vegetables. The headteacher's wife also provided me with vegetables at times. One day,

I helped her dig in her garden. I asked for a portion to make my own vegetable beds. I had a sturdy supply of vegetables. I even gave some to her, while selling others. Hard work pays; even a skill such as growing vegetables can help improve our lives.

Initially, I was allocated accommodation in a distant area known as the Fisheries: a farming community of different tribal groups, complete with fish dams. It was about five kilometres from the school. Each morning, I left my house to cycle towards the mountains where the school was; and made the journey back in the afternoon.

This was not safe at all, as the place was infested with liberation fighters. I explained this to the farm manager, so they could move me closer to the school. There was accommodation available, but they were adamant. It was only when a landmine blew up near the place where I used to live, killing a veterinary doctor, that they took action. I was relocated to the bachelors' mess, where management used to live. This was a posh area: all amenities were of high standard, because only white people and the farm manager used to live there. I was given a very neatly thatched round house with an outside small thatched kitchen. There was even a swimming pool. This was like a dream come true.

I even asked my mother to come and visit me, because now she could sleep in a comfortable bed, unlike in the other accommodation. She came with my sister; the first time she had ever come to Harare. I could see her excitement from the many questions she asked. As we were living among white people, she was more fascinated. Such a scenario was unheard of. Previously, my mother's only experience of anyone white was when my great grandfather had been invited to become leader of the village.

As she was walking outside in my backyard, she saw a white woman over the fence wearing a bikini and laying down by the poolside. She flew back into the house making intense physical gestures and with a questioning eye. She asked how a woman could walk about naked in public. It took several attempts to convince her that it was their culture and there was nothing immoral about it. This clash of cultures was a norm in Zimbabwe at the time, permeating the roots of black people's dislike of white men.

At Henderson, I had another encounter with the ugly face of the liberation war. I was cycling to school one day when I saw a burning tractor by the roadside. It had been hit by a landmine; the driver was stuck in his burning machine. I could tell from afar that he was struggling. From stories I had heard earlier, I knew it was very dangerous to approach any burning vehicle: not just because of the obvious danger of it blowing up, but in the surrounding area, those who had planted the mine could be lying in wait. I was scared to death from both dangers, but something inside me kept on nagging to help this driver.

Quickly, I threw my bike to one side, and ran stealthily towards the burning tractor. The driver's leg was lodged deep into the damaged front where the landmine had hit, making it very difficult to pull him out. I tried harder, praying I got through this without any harm to both of us, as there could be guns looming in the vicinity. Finally, I managed to pull out Mr Tembo, who I identified as a well-known driver at Henderson.

Now, there was a further danger of becoming publicly known as his rescuer. After pulling him out, I made sure he was in a safe place far from the tractor and ran back to my bike to disappear from the scene. His leg was badly damaged, as the landmine had hit him along with the front of his tractor. To this day, nobody from Henderson knows about the person who rescued him; I have only ever shared it with my wife. His leg was later amputated: after which he retired from his duties. The secret of who saved him died with him years later.

During the same period, I was staying with two of my nephews, Cosmas (from my brother's side), and Cuthbert (from my sister's side), who were attending the school I worked at. Another nephew, Morris, Cuthbert's brother, had started secondary education at Mazowe Secondary Boarding School, the same as I had attended. He was now in Form 3. It was the end of term: Morris and Cuthbert would both go home to the rural areas to be with their mother. Their father was in prison at the time. I took them to the bus station, so they could catch the earliest bus to Chawanda, our rural home in Mount Darwin. They would disembark at Chakuveza, just a few kilometres from my own home in Chawanda. My sister's home and her husband's business were in Chakuveza. It was a walking distance from my home.

Just as the bus was approaching Karoyi River, it was ambushed by liberation fighters, who had been hiding in the bushes. Everyone was asked to get off the bus and follow them. This was now a trend in recruiting more people to fight in the struggle for independence. The fighters would round up people wherever they were gathered - or waylay them in unsuspected areas. Many, young and old, joined the war in this way. They had to walk for days to the training camps in Chimoio, Mozambique.

On this fateful day, Morris and Cuthbert were both on the bus and among those who were going to be taken across the border. They had only travelled a few kilometres when they realised Cuthbert was too young for recruitment into the guerrilla war. They then asked him to find his way home, which he did: but he also brought the news that Morris had gone. This was devastating news for my sister, who spent many months afterwards believing that her first-born child had gone for ever. Many parents experienced this; most of those recruited for war were young and of school-going age.

However, unbeknownst to all of us, Morris was very interested in joining the war. There had been a great deal of activism at Mazowe Secondary School. Many young people risked their lives in Chimurenga guerrilla warfare. We later learnt about Morris' journey when he returned home during the ceasefire. The war was won; Zimbabwe had been granted independence. When Morris came home, he had assumed the life of a fighter and was stubborn: choosing to smoke and parade himself as an ex-combatant. These people had instilled fear in many - so when they came back, that fear remained.

As godfather to Morris, my aim was that he obtained an education, which he resisted at first. It was me who had ensured he got to secondary school when his father was in jail, so he had to listen. I was quite forceful. He had to budge in the end. I encouraged him to study and bought him lectures to read by correspondence. He took this stage of his life seriously and went on to complete his 'O' Levels with flying colours. From there, nothing would stop him. I am so glad he took my advice and is now a success.

I remained at Henderson, where my accommodation again changed: this time, to a three-room cottage, back-to-back with another family. One of their daughters, who used to help me with cleaning and laundry, became Morris' wife.

Maybe the most difficult thing about my time at Henderson was how dead things were socially. I was frightened by the environment, such were the stories coming from the community. One of the scariest was that certain people on the farm could use juju and black magic to abuse people. One of these stories held that if we lent people money in the community, they could take the rest by black magic. I was therefore advised not to lend money to anybody.

Another story had it that if someone took any of the daughters off the farm, they would forever remain there. Many young men who came to work there after finishing their agricultural training married there. During my 7 years there as a teacher, I noticed how many families let their daughters all but force themselves on young men. They ended up marrying prematurely.

I rescued a friend who had just come to work as an assistant farm manager. He was targeted and had to pay the family of someone who had forced herself on him. Most of those who did this wanted money and to get a son-in-law who was well to do.

Meanwhile, guerillas continued to advance across the surrounding farms. The farm authorities insisted that young men like me should go into national service to defend the country. I was nearly co-opted into this; but saved by the ceasefire declared in 1978-9. When freedom fighters arrived on the farm, one tractor driver was killed by a landmine. With the farm now under siege, all residents were monitored: ensuring they could not feed or come into direct contact with the fighters.

*My last days at Henderson*

In my final days at Henderson, I was involved in an accident and lost one of my upper front teeth. The school head seemed to have targeted me and wanted me to go. Yet there were moments of happiness too. Due to the shortage of accommodation in the school, the Farm Superintendent offered me a one bedroom thatched flat. I lived in this house for a year. It was a real privilege, as it was electrified: which I did not need to pay for. One day, I planned to own my own home with the same amenities; and went on to do so.

During my stay at the Research Station, I enjoyed the cheap milk, eggs, honey and light which we received. Yet the whole place fell into an increasingly alarming state of disrepair due to the rapidly deteriorating political situation in Zimbabwe. It was destroyed. I left to start a new life, in the conviction that I could start a family if I remained.

Yet in those final days before my departure, something terrifying almost destroyed everything. One day, Gallie was with me. While we slept, a snake appeared from the ceiling. It descended slowly. I did not see its head. It continued coming down and with a bang, it fell on our bed. All hell broke loose. I jumped up and escaped through the window. I screamed for Gallie to follow. The whole episode was made worse by a radio cable which had entangled itself around my legs. It is an incident I will never forget. The strangest thing was the teacher who replaced me when I had left saw a real snake in her house too. She also had to leave the school.

## A new home

I now had a car of my own. I had bought a house in an affluent suburb in Mabelreign as a joint project with Jerome. When I planned to marry Gallie, he was already married to Benhilda. By coincidence, our wives had been friends since primary school. Much as we would have loved to stay together in the same house and divide the rooms, this proved difficult. Both our wives were still in school; but each time they were in the house together, it became tense. The friction proved too much when out of jealousy, my friend brought my former girlfriend to our home. This was intended to make my young wife uncomfortable, and even provoke her to leave me. It did not work, as I had told Gallie everything about my past. She loved me far too deeply to be affected by this - but it made me realise the need for our own place.

An opportunity came up to buy a house, where my friend's mother-in-law was working as a housekeeper in Hatfield. I went to view this house with Gallie while we were still dating and on the verge of marriage. She liked it. It was in a big yard compared to the one I had bought with my friend. It was not that presentable. It was built in the 1950s and had plenty of wear and tear. Nonetheless, we saw its potential, and loved the idea of growing our own vegetables and crops at the back of the yard.

We made arrangements to buy it from Mr Wilson, the owner. He was South African and planning to go back home. The transaction stalled when I was trying to raise the deposit for the mortgage. As a civil servant, I could obtain a mortgage; but the amount required of 1500 dollars was very difficult to come by. A teacher's salary in 1982 was around 300 dollars. Given that I was preparing dowry for my wife, luck was not on my side at this point.

About six months elapsed between saving for the deposit and my last conversation with Mr Wilson. One day, Gallie had just come from school and immediately walked straight into the house we were living in. She connected the phone, which was always disconnected from the wall to discourage overuse. This was my friend's idea of how to save money.

On this lucky day, Gallie wanted to call me as she did every Friday to check whether I would be coming home over the weekend. The moment she plugged the phone in, it rang; at the other end of the line was Mr Wilson. He had been trying to reach me to find out if I was still interested in the house, and this this was the last call: he was putting it back on the market. Gallie quickly told him that we were still interested and she would call me straightaway. When she gave me the news, I promptly called Mr Wilson to give him my firm confirmation that I would be bringing the deposit the following Monday. As promised, I saw him and paid the deposit. We went together to sign the papers at the lawyers, Honey and Bleckenburg. On 12 August 1982, we moved to our new house and left Mabelreign. This would become our long-term home.

When we moved in, our neighbour, Mr Mandaza, came peeping through the windows: which had no curtains, as we could not afford any! We had moved in with the bare minimum. We were very happy; and Gallie was pregnant with our first child, Mavreen.

## St Manocks and Kutsaga Research Station School

By now, Gallie and I were married. I decided to leave Henderson for a school closer to Harare, where I had now purchased my own home. The transfer process into inner Harare was a struggle: many qualifying teachers had chosen to teach in the big city. Unfortunately, the Ministry of Education did not accept a rural teacher into urban schools. Thus, I had to remain in schools near Harare.

After many visits to the Ministry of Education and applications to different schools, I obtained a position to teach Grade 5 at St Manocks School in January 1983, just a few months before Mavreen was born; and subsequently, moved on to Kutsaga. Most of my teaching years were spent at the latter, which faced almost the same perils as Henderson. Tea and transport were subsidised. I managed to prosper and improve my education. My children grew up well and my wife realised her goals too. The only disappointing thing was that promotion was not available, so I remained a dedicated primary school teacher.

St Manocks, moreover, was also a farm school: administered by Windmill, a fertiliser company. It was a good school with many benefits, some of which included rationing of food hampers at the end of each month. We also had the opportunity to go into the fields after the potato harvest to pick any leftovers. This was a hugely interesting experience: many women filled entire buckets and sold them to other neighbouring farms. The chicken runs at the farm provided another delicacy; we picked chicken legs after they were slaughtered.

We had a beautiful life at St Manocks, commuting between Harare and Mt Hampden where the school was. However, it proved short-lived. On one of our football outings, I met an old friend: who told me he was leaving his school in Harare to move closer to home in Murehwa,

Mashonaland East. A replacement for him had yet to be found. I went for an interview - and the next thing I knew, was moving my young family from St Manocks to our house in Harare, as I had been given the job by the Governing Body of Katanga Research Station School, another one just like Henderson.

Kutsaga was one of the most renowned tobacco research stations in the world. The school there catered for a small number of employees' children and some families in Epworth. I started there in January 1984; and remained until 2002 when I left for the UK. I moved upwards through the ranks: from class teacher, senior teacher, Deputy Head to Acting Head, a position I held until my application to study abroad. My house was a few miles from the school, so the benefits included provision of transport, to and from work. A van would pick me up near my home each morning. This meant I did not use my car regularly; but left it for my wife who needed it most.

She was now teaching at a secondary school, Cranborne Boys High School, in Harare. By now, we had two more children: Tawanda Malvern, born in September 1985; and Takudzwa Marilyn, born seven years after Tawanda. We were a complete family by then and decided against another child, even though my wife was still very young. We decided on this after she had gone through caesarean section for all three children. I did not want her to suffer again. I had three beautiful children that God had given us.

We became the pillar of both extended families, supporting them financially and in times of need. We were the only family with an open-door policy to accommodate everyone. They all used to come unannounced. Even though this strained our resources, we were ready to help. On one winter's day, we had a number of visitors who, as usual, did not have blankets with them. My wife and I ended up using only a bed sheet to cover ourselves because we gave all our blankets to the visitors! There were many such occasions, but at least some were during summer.

Our lives remained like this for many years to come. News went around that my wife was very hospitable; even distant, faraway relatives came to share in this generosity. A cousin of mine also passed word around that my wife would let him serve himself at the table, meaning he could choose the chicken pieces he liked. This was his motivation.

As someone who knew, first-hand, the value of education in eradicating poverty, I took it upon myself to support my extended family in this regard. However, I failed in my endeavour: not because I did not know how, but most were not willing to submit to education. My call was heard mostly by my sisters' families, whose children took heed. My brothers' children did not see the logic in what I was saying; and instead saw me as the one who should provide for them, as I had all the resources to do so.

This mentality raised a whole generation dependent on my family. Entire families looked to me for assistance in everything. At my wife's request, I took one of my brother's daughters to stay with us and help her through secondary school in Harare. We got her a very highly regarded school in Chitungwiza. Zengeza 1 High School was one of the best schools in the area, churning out students who moved on to prestigious universities.

Phoebe braved it to Form 3, after which she fell head over heels in love. Despite all our efforts to encourage her to complete her studies, she was adamant. The situation was made worse by her mother who, unbeknown to us, was busily encouraging her daughter to get married. Her pressure succeeded, very much to the detriment of her daughter's future. Phoebe got married, but her husband later contracted AIDS. Theirs became a life of agony, with her husband having to leave work regularly when contracting different infections.

Phoebe regrets her decision, especially when she sees the fruits of education in my own children. Mavreen, my eldest daughter, had to help her send her children to school after observing the hardship she was going through to balance a sick husband and raising school fees. I thank my daughter for her compassion; but also for recognising that the best thing she could help her cousin with was getting her children educated. They were so to university level and Gerald, the younger one, later won a scholarship to study Actuarial Science at NAST University in Bulawayo.

We also supported my brother's youngest daughter, after she failed her 'O' levels. She had to repeat these before proceeding on to her 'A' levels. Fortunately, she passed, and was able to enrol at the local school for her sixth form studies. She progressed quite well - but little did we know that our intention of seeing her move on to university would again be thwarted. She found love soon after completing high school and her mother, again, saw fit to encourage her into marriage. Ivy is now languishing with a child whose father is a self-proclaimed trader.

However, Herbert, my other niece's son, who started the journey together with Ivy and was also supported by us, braved it out, and is now studying Accounting and Finance at the University of Chinhoyi. All this only further proves the agony suffered by female children in Zimbabwe and, indeed, Africa. They are viewed as a commodity which can be sold. What so many parents are not aware of is that marriage unsupported by personal growth through education will throw girls into a future of uncertainty: where they are abused by the same men who had purported to love them.

Sadly, all my brothers' children are living lives of dependence, leaving them despising those who have become successful through education. It has always been my dream to see people getting an education and obtaining the fruits of success. Education removes people from the chains of poverty and dependency. It enlightens and opens new horizons to an abundance of opportunities around the world. It is because of education that I see myself and my family among the most respected in our community. Thanks to this respect, when we talk, people listen; they value our opinion. Education empowers and liberates; it is a passport to a better future.

During the war, young people were recruited to go abroad and obtain an education. They had to be sneaked out of the country via Botswana or Mozambique. Some of my friends escaped through these routes with the help of guerrilla fighters. Their education helped them secure positions in government after the struggle was over. I was unaffected by this, as I remained focused on my teaching. At the time, going abroad was not an option for me; and later, when the opportunity to travel to the UK to follow my wife presented itself, I was initially somewhat hesitant.

What motivated me to go at last was that I was also going to further my education. Education is the true story of my life. It has given me a sense of achievement and freedom. My three children are highly qualified with advanced university degrees, earning them good jobs. We might say that opportunities availed themselves to my children given their educated parents - but they were also availed to my extended family who alas, did not take them.

While at Kutsaga, I studied for my postgraduate diploma. I enjoyed my job and was the envy of most of my colleagues. I lived in a low-density area and had a car. The children went to boarding school. In 2002, however, I took the plunge, and followed my wife to the UK.

# CHAPTER 3:

# SETTLING IN THE UNITED KINGDOM

My entry into the UK was dramatic and eventful. I had my two children on the plane: which had taken us all the way to Gatwick Airport. As we hovered above the British mainland, I was fascinated by the beautiful green scenery below me. I had the small Salvation Army hymn book, which I had read through the flight. We eventually touched ground and taxied to the area where we were going to alight. My children were happy, but nobody spoke. They must have seen how scared I was by the look on my face. As a father, I had to be strong. I called on God to intervene and our ancestors to support me and give me strength.

We filed up through the arrival area and got to the immigration suite. We presented our passports and waited for the next step. The officer politely asked me to state my reason for travelling to the UK. I did so: which led to a series of activities. The first was a mini detention, after I said my children and I were seeking asylum. The officers led us to a holding area. All the passengers were cleared. Our group remained until we were led to another immigration area, where I was interrogated. My English was perfect; with confidence, I provided all the answers. I told them why I had come and my intentions in the future. It was a sad situation back home. I was showing all the signs of suffering as a parent. My children were not malnourished, but they did not look their best.

The immigration process took the whole night. We surrendered our passports, went through medical tests and further questioning about my previous employment. Our luggage was inspected; at the end of the whole process, we were given travel papers. Our entry into the UK was finally granted. My older daughter had travelled through the night from Sunderland and was there at Gatwick waiting for us, thanks to my clever wife: who had planned our entry in advance through a lawyer. Everything had been easy for us because she had engaged a lawyer to facilitate our entry.

As we left Gatwick on 2 July 2002, a new chapter in our lives would start. The weather was not what we had expected. It was freezing; though for my daughter, who had been there for a while, it was summer. We wrapped our thin coats around us as we went to the bus station with our suitcases. The immigration staff had asked us if we had any accommodation while processing our papers. We told them my wife was already here, so she would accommodate us. They agreed to this.

We travelled to Sunderland, a journey of five hours from London. What a culture shock we experienced! The scenery was beautiful, with green plains that looked like they were demarcated naturally. These, I later realised, were farming areas. Takudzwa, who was eight at the time, had many questions; but I could not give her answers, as I was also trying to get to grips with our new environment.

We arrived in Sunderland very late at night and went straight to my wife's apartment. She was living in a two-bed flat owned by Sunderland University, where she was in her final year studying for a Master's in Education. The space was enough to accommodate all of us as a family. The girls used the spare bedroom, where my older daughter had been staying. Tawanda, our son, slept downstairs on the sofa bed. This was very convenient for us. We were close to all amenities and could walk to town on foot.

I did so the following morning when accompanying my wife to catch a bus to work. It was quite a trek to the bus station: where she took a bus to Peterlee, where her school was. I thought I was clever enough to know my directions back to the flat but alas, it took me more than four hours to get back after getting lost in town. I had to call my daughter for assistance. What a start!

As I discovered, Sunderland had started to become a more cosmopolitan city, boasting many people from different countries. The student population was why; they were from all over the world. A city which had hitherto suffered from lack of diversity was now bustling with many nationalities. However, Sunderland still had pockets where people suffered racial discrimination. The government responded to a call from a South African dancing group which had experienced discrimination while touring the city. The story was all over the newspapers; leading to a government directive to accommodate any newcomers to the area. Many refugees and asylum seekers were sent there, and the student population soared.

We settled in our little place happily. Through discussions with others in the same predicament, I learnt that I could receive benefits as an asylum seeker. We were shown offices which would provide these benefits. To my amazement, they could offer a larger accommodation space, a weekly family allowance, free electricity, water and so on. Immediately, we moved from Pans Bank, where my wife's university accommodation was located, to a four-bedroom house in Midfield. This was already furnished. Oh, what a shock! We had enough bedrooms to accommodate even the two young people who had come to join us from Zimbabwe.

One of them was Nancy Ziyenge, who stayed with my wife as a stepping-stone en route to remaining permanently in the UK. She was my daughter's age and lived on the same street in Hatfield. Her parents had asked if Gallie could accommodate her. Nancy was just like our daughter. Kudzai Munongi, meanwhile, travelled with us from Zimbabwe as a way of helping his parents. He was also like a son, though older than all our children. This new space could accommodate all of us.

On 14 August 2002, I was called to Liverpool for an interview, where I was granted refugee status. My wife accompanied me. It was a good trip. Our train fares and accommodation had been paid for. We stayed in a hotel, a walking distance from the offices we would go for the interview. Having walked around in the early morning to get a feel of Liverpool, we headed towards the offices. My interview was scheduled for 11am. We sat in the waiting room and when it was my turn, I was invited in; my wife was not allowed to join me. After about an hour of interrogation through rigorous questioning, I came out, exhausted. I had gone through a nightmare. What I discovered during this interview was the need to remain consistent. I was asked the same question repeatedly, in an attempt to confuse me.

On 21 August 2002, I received a letter stating I had been granted leave to remain in the UK, which brought an immense sense of relief to the family. We could now look for employment or to further our education. This was a good beginning for Tawanda, Takudzwa and I. As for my wife and eldest daughter, who had been in the country before us, another series of appointments with a lawyer led to us finally being united.

## My first experiences in Sunderland

Initially, I had the ambition to become a primary school teacher, just like back home in Zimbabwe. Yet my first day as a supply teacher was something of a disaster. I remember arriving at the school in Hebburn after travelling for an hour on two different metros. I found the headteacher in her office, where I introduced myself. Quickly, she took me to my cover class for that day and introduced me to them in haste, as though she wanted to leave as fast as possible.

The pupils looked at me with utter amazement, sizing me up to see if I was strong enough to withstand the emotional abuse I would subsequently experience from them. To me, they looked innocent, just like any other primary schoolkids. What I did not know was that behind that innocence lurked strong undercurrents of rudeness and mischief.

After I had introduced myself, the drama started with a red-haired girl, who stood up to ask me something in an accent I failed to understand. This was a two-sided problem, as the students could not understand me either. The nightmare began when pupils stood up and said something which was opposed by half the class. This went on for some time. I had not even introduced the lesson when I realised half an hour had passed. By the time I did introduce it, it was almost time to start a new one.

Then one girl stood up, opened a can of Coca-Cola and leapt onto the table. Upon opening the fizzy drink, it hissed out of the can onto her classmates' faces. I was confused; thrown by what was happening. I started speaking in Shona and some pupils accused me of swearing. I wore a murderous face and called everybody to order, lest there would be dire consequences.

Again, some children accused me of being harsh. The good ones who behaved moderately suggested calling in the headteacher. I could not do this, as it would represent utter failure on my part. I had taught in three Zimbabwe primary schools for over 20 years. I had to regain order; with tact and strategy, I won over three-quarters of the class, lessons resumed; but later, I walked into the head's office and told her I was leaving and would not be returning to the school.

This was quite the start to my working life in the UK! In some respects, it ended my passion for teaching the primary level curriculum I had enjoyed for 25 years; but it would also open up new opportunities in alternative education with young and disengaged people.

The UK has an open educational culture which welcomes everyone who wants to learn, young or old. I enrolled for a Master's degree in Gender, Culture and Development. This programme helped train me and view life as a human rights activist. Through the course, I learnt about the impact of gender stereotypes on women; the concepts of race, ethnicity and the oppression of certain peoples, such as homosexuals. I recognised the differences between the culture in which I had grown up and that of Europe. Cultures differ in very many ways; I had much to learn and absorb.

I also studied feminism in depth. Patriarchy had taught me to view women as an 'other': namely, that they 'belonged' to men. Through learning and research, I gained vital insight into the need to close this gender stereotype.

I also needed to take responsibility for our youngest daughter, who was still in primary school. She needed to be dropped off and picked up from school, wholly unlike in Zimbabwe. During my school years, I'd had to walk several kilometres to school from the tender age of six. We used to cover long distances; sometimes, I risked my life crossing flooded rivers, just to get to school. Yet through persistence and perseverance, this difficult start made me the man I am now.

I really enjoyed dropping off and picking up my daughter. It brought me joy to know that she was safe. My other two children were grown up, studying and working, so did not have time to help with the school errands. My wife, meanwhile, was working a nine to five job. The school was a couple of kilometres from where we lived, so required a bus. As time went by, I would put my daughter on the bus and wait for her at the bus stop when she came back.

This was just before she started going to secondary school: a Catholic, girls only school. When she started there, she had no issues getting on and off the Metro with friends. She had made many friends at junior school, who accompanied her into high school. They used to walk in groups, which I found very reassuring. There were one or two occasions, though, when she encountered some hooligans who harassed her, and she had to be rescued by friends or passers-by.

When we started living in Sunderland, black and other minority people had just started doing so *en masse* too. Many had sought asylum from war-torn countries. The majority of the city's inhabitants had not seen a black person before then; when it dawned on them that they were receiving some form of benefit, which they themselves did not have, they reacted with negativity to the newcomers: throwing all sorts of abuse at anyone who happened to be nearby, verbal or physical.

I cannot say, though, that Sunderland did not feel like home - because that would be a lie. The Salvation Army, Sunderland Monkwearmouth Corps, effectively became our second home. My wife, having been the first to come, made links with the Corps and later formed lasting relationships with the elderly people there. Some of them took it upon themselves to look after us and invited us for lunches on Sundays.

For many years, this continued with a particular family, the Loshes: John and Grace. It was now their and our tradition to have lunch on Sundays at their house. They took us in as part of their family and made sure we had all we needed. They even bought the first uniforms for my two children when they first enrolled in school. They facilitated accommodation and furniture for us before we later bought our own house.

Even after we moved away from Sunderland, we remained part of the Salvation Army; and go back there to worship every time we visit from the UAE, where we live now. My children have gone to join other churches; but for my wife and I, Sunderland Monkwearmouth Salvation Army will always be our worshipping home, where we received spiritual and material support in those early days. We have seen people come and go and others passing on. It is our spiritual home.

Those early years in Sunderland were the 'make or break' period for me and my family: when we established another set of roots, but in a foreign country. As I started looking for a job, opportunities presented themselves. To begin with, my wife encouraged me to go for a teaching job after a short volunteering stint at my daughter's former primary school. Having taught in Zimbabwe, it did not cost me anything to get a job in the UK. I am a dedicated worker with a powerful CV and a progressive mentality. Thus I first got a job as a homework guide. I worked at a school where I could guide young people in research and completing their homework.

My problem was using computers. I could not navigate them to find what I was looking for. The young people guided me instead. Beyond this issue, I had the knowledge needed to successfully help these young people research for information. I enjoyed the job and my manager was very understanding.

My next permanent job opportunity came with a government agency, Connexions. This is when my passion to help young achievers was rekindled. I worked with a group of young people in neither education, employment nor training, who needed activities to keep them engaged: thereby reducing offending and re-offending rates. They were very vulnerable people with little or no skills to cope in their personal lives. Some of them ended up in prison because of drug-related offences. My levels of empathy greatly increased after realising they could be engaged by something positive: improving their lives and re-connecting with society. This was a very rewarding experience.

On one occasion, a young person I was working with, Paul, glimpsed the police from a distance and immediately thought they were looking for him. He started running along the road, oblivious to the cars speeding along it. His aim was to run as far away as possible. At that moment, the police saw him and ran after him, making matters worse. They were not running after him to arrest him; but to make sure he was safe on such a busy road. I was very concerned about his safety, and hugely relieved when they caught up with him and explained their intentions. Observing these young people's problems impacted greatly on ensuring my own kids did not go through the same sorts of experiences.

When we left Zimbabwe, we appreciated that only education could provide opportunities in the UK. My kids took heed of my and my wife's advice. They embarked on study routes which led all three to obtain university education. The youngest, Takudzwa, left Zimbabwe when she was only 9; and completed her primary, high school and university education in the UK. She was so accustomed to her new environment that her integration was smooth. She would even criticise the family whenever we spoke about racism. She would defend her white friends: who were the majority compared to blacks.

Takudzwa's views were Western, albeit she could speak our language and eat our type of food. All three assimilated Western values to an extent; though for the two older ones, the values they grew up believing were predominant in their everyday interactions. Tawanda went on to specialise in Estate Management and Tariro, the eldest, studied Social Work. My children made us very proud by obtaining these qualifications and going on to better employment prospects: especially in a Western setting.

As a family trying to establish new roots in a new country, sticking together and braving these challenges was our first priority. We lived together with our teenagers and young child: first in rented accommodation, then securing a mortgage to buy our own house. This was a great achievement; with both parents working, it made a big difference in how we were viewed by friends and acquaintances. That we are a God-fearing couple, who made sure that attendance at church was a weekly routine, led many people in Sunderland, young and old, to look up to us for advice.

I became a personal adviser; not only to young people, but also with families arriving in Sunderland from elsewhere, in terms of employment and training opportunities. I was now involved with many organisations, and part of major meetings happening in the education and employment fields, including funding options for young people.

Yet it was not all a bed of roses. There were challenges in working with young people of this nature. They brought with them many social problems: including lack of skills, offending behaviour and forming relationships. While working in this role, I was approached by management to join a university programme sponsored by the organisation. I was the only one who met the entry requirements for a Diploma in Personal Advising.

## The Leazes

By this time, we had moved home twice. We lived in another house in Hendon. It was a bit far from the schools my son and daughter were attending; though my son was old enough to make his way by himself, as he had now been accepted to study 'A' Level at a boy's only Catholic school. This became our routine for a couple of months, until we moved to our new home on Hylton Road. We could afford our own place, as my wife was in a good job. We bought it after looking for a better area where we would not suffer any racial abuse and be among other professional people. My wife wanted a big house outside the city area; but I felt this would create many problems for us as a family. We later agreed on a house near the city and university.

The Leazes, in Millfield, was the best choice we ever made. It was small but perfect for our family, dwindling in size now our older daughter had moved out. It is in a quiet area, walking distance from the town centre and near many amenities, including Millfield metro station.

Millfield became our home and community. Our two children continued their schooling from there. Towanda was at St Aidan's and Takudzwa was now at St Anthony's, both Catholic high schools considered the best in the area. We bought the house in March 2004; but good planners that we are, thought of investing in another property, a bigger one this time. In the local newspaper, we spotted a house very close to The Leazes, with all the features we were looking for in an investment. It was a four-bedroom house: exactly what someone would wish for in a secluded area in Millfield. It was in a cul-de-sac; there were only 19 houses in that plot. My wife saw it first and commented that we could see ourselves living there.

We both fell in love with it and arranged a viewing with the estate agent. It looked quite unkempt, with a lot of debris and worn out floors with carpets ripped off. The owners, who were going through a divorce, had not given it much care. Yet this worked in our favour, as the price was reduced. We could see potential beyond the state of the house, even though we were heavily criticised by our children. We bought it all the same.

We turned 9 Arrol Park into a beautiful place, which we are proud of to this day. We later converted the garage into a ground floor bedroom; so now, it has five bedrooms. We worked on these different projects over time and our patience paid off. We still consider Arrol Park our family home, even when we are outside the country. All our kids grew up there and went their own ways, leaving the nest empty. They still come back home.

We managed to rent out The Leazes to students; this helped us pay the mortgage. We have had no problems renting it out because of its location. It was a fantastic choice.

## The prophecy became real

When I was growing up, I barely envisaged travelling abroad. I did think of leaving for Northern Rhodesia, now Zambia, but that never happened. I did not have the confidence to realise my potential due to a poor family background. I often admired those who made it abroad. Later on, I became rather graceless: failing to admire those who had gone overseas and come back home. Most had nothing to show for it apart from boasting about making white girlfriends or taking drugs and grifting. That was wrong; in fact, many people had succeeded in many fields while staying, working or learning in countries such as the UK.

I strongly believe that dreams come true. Of course, the opportunity to move to the UK arose through my wife - but the strange thing about it was a prediction by my late sister, years previously, about Gallie studying abroad. She prophesised that she was going to prosper: predicting this while possessed by a spirit which all our family believed in.

As all her previous predictions had come to pass, my sister became the powerhouse in our family. Whatever she said was accepted as the truth. She was called Ennia, and possessed by the spirit of our ancestor, Chikowore. Although she was married and had her own children, she continued performing the duties of our spirit medium, much to the chagrin of her in-laws. However, they had to respect this. Ennia would be called at any time to perform these duties by the family. Each time my family and I would visit the rural area, we would pass by her village to have the spiritual anointing, so our journey would be safe.

At one time, when my wife was expecting our first child, my sister predicted she would have a caesarean section and hence should go to her family: where she would receive support during pregnancy as well as after delivery. Also, as custom demands, when a newly married wife is pregnant with her first child, she must be taken back to her family through a process called 'kusungira'. Soon after the child is born, another process, 'kutara', will be performed: the husband's family sends a representative, normally an aunt, to take gifts for the in-laws, thanking them for looking after their wife during and after pregnancy. This is when the wife and baby are brought back to the family.

As per Ennia's prediction, my wife indeed had a caesarean section to deliver our first child. The complication was called 'placenta praevia', the disengagement of the placenta from the uterus just as labour begins. This is a life-threatening condition; my wife needed an emergency C-section to save her and the child's lives. Initially, the doctors thought the baby was no more, and their priority was to save the mother. However, they found the baby alive when they opened the mother. This is how our daughter, named Tariro (Hope) by my mother-in-law, got her name. My sister had been right.

She also predicted that my wife would go abroad where the white men are and would be the family bread winner. A year later, Gallie got a scholarship to study in the UK. Our settling there was the happiest event in the history of the Kawanzaruwa family. My wife became a pillar of success for our immediate and extended families. She provided spiritual and financial support; everyone benefitted from her generosity. I remember her collecting 52 suitcases of clothes sent to Zimbabwe for family and the immediate community. She donated to the Salvation Army and collected musical instruments to be used by the Army Corps in Hatfield, Harare.

Then my wife won a contract to work for three years in the United Arab Emirates (UAE). She was going to work for the Ministry of Education there. This was a challenge, as I had to be with her. I had a good job, which I had vowed to keep and retire in. I told my managers about it, and they allowed me sabbatical leave for three years. Having agreed on this, I left my job: I never returned to it. Instead, I went to the Middle East, and settled there; but never worked as previously anticipated, as my situation became affected by various other events, which the next chapter explains.

# CHAPTER 4:

# THE UAE AND DECLINING HEALTH

While in the UAE, my UK status changed. As I was serving my three-year sabbatical, it was announced by my employers that I could take early retirement, as I was about to turn 55. I complied, collected my dues and left my job. I continued to live with my wife in the UAE. I applied for jobs until she told me to stay at home. I was approaching 60 and enjoying good health. At first, I thought this was unfair as I had much still to do and wanted to contribute to the family bread basket. My wife and children discouraged me from thinking of going back to work; ultimately, I conceded they were right.

Ras Al Khaimah was our first port of call in the UAE: where we were welcomed as educators, Gallie especially. All seven Emirates are part of the federal entity, with Abu Dhabi the federal capital. The fascinating bit is that the capital of each Emirate is the name of each too. As we settled in RAK, it became apparent that we had come to a very different part of the world, which contrasted greatly to the Zimbabwean or British environments we knew and were used to. The culture was that of a religious community, where the call to prayer is emphasised and followed. It is a Muslim country, in which religion is steeped in culture and tradition; a respectful way of living maintained for many years. The Emirati dress code is an abbaya, with a shayla for women and kandura for men. I even bought one for myself. The people were kind and very generous.

## Al Ain

Al Ain is part of Abu Dhabi, well known for its rich underground water springs: a main reason the area was settled in originally. It still uses the ancient falaj system to irrigate many areas by passing water through a network of tunnels and open channels. Al Ain was originally known as Tawam and Al Buraimi oasis; the current name of the city means 'water spring'.

The majority of the city's residents are Indian subcontinental expatriates, mainly from Pakistan. Teeming with parks, roundabouts and foliage-lined streets, the city is often referred to as the 'Garden City of the Gulf'. Camel racing and breeding are both traditional activities, giving an insight into Al Ain's cultural past. Visitors can view this traditional form of commerce at the Camel Souq each day.

Al Ain is home to a large fort, built to protect the city from raiders. It was Sheikh Zayed's base before he rose to prominence as Sheikh of Abu Dhabi. There are numerous other forts in different states of reconstruction scattered throughout the city and its outlying areas, which showcase its long and varied past. Many of these forts have been excavated; some are open to the public for viewing.

Inhabited for over 4,000 years, Al Ain is the fourth largest city in the country, with over 370,000 residents. Positioned just adjacent to Oman's western border, the freeway between Dubai, Abu Dhabi and Al Ain connect in the centre of the country to form a triangle, with each city approximately 130 km apart. Until September 14, 2006, the border crossing between Oman and Al Ain was open. Since then, however, it has remained closed, and now requires those wishing to cross to clear immigration when entering and exiting.

We found ourselves resident in this rich Emirate between 2011 and 2014, a time we will forever cherish. Al Ain brings back good memories. We had a good time there. My wife had secured a position to work in the Institute of Applied Technology as Deputy Director, Academic. It was a girl's only school that catered for only local students. It was a rich institution, which provided students with free education, laptops and iPads. It was my first experience of such support for children's education.

When Gallie joined, the school needed revamping. Part of a group of schools, it had to be aligned to the whole system through accreditation. My wife took it on to real prominence during her time there. We stayed in a villa with two bedrooms. Her job was well paid. I remember meeting an elderly man every morning when I went to buy the local newspaper. We later became friends; how, I really don't know. We spoke very different languages, but it seemed we understood each other. We became very good friends in the end and language was not a barrier.

Healthwise, I was not in a good position in Al Ain. My sinus problem, which had gradually been developing for quite some time, became worse. I had a number of visits to the nose, throat and ears specialist, with no resolution. I'd had an operation a year beforehand; but it made the growths worse, to the detriment of my overall health. The operation had been performed in Ras Al Khaimah; I consulted the specialist there, but he could do no more for me.

I walked every night with my wife to try and get into shape and improve our health. This did help; but my breathing was laboured, as I had developed mild asthma. It was becoming a nightmare. We ended up buying nebulisers to help with the condition. This was the beginning of my health scare whish tormented me for years.

We left Al Ain after another opportunity availed itself in Ras Al Khaimah at the school owned by the Sheikh (Prince). My wife was to be the Director there and it was an amazing opportunity, almost beyond belief.

## The Emirate of Ras Al Khaimah

Ras Al Khaimah boasts an impressive archaeological heritage and rich, cultural history. Its enticing combination of fertile plains, scenic mountains, white beaches, mangroves and desert landscapes have lured settlers for seven millennia, making it one of the oldest continuously inhabited regions on Earth.

Ras Al Khaimah's strategic location at the mouth of the Arabian Gulf has always oriented it towards economic and cultural exchange. Archaeological investigations demonstrate that trade has been an essential part of life in the area since at least 5000 BC. Since then, Ras Al Khaimah has variously been named Julfar, Majan and Al Seer, and was widely known throughout the Gulf for its commercial activity. By the 10th century AD, inhabitants of Ras Al Khaimah routinely travelled as far afield as Zanzibar, Bombay, and China.

Ras Al Khaimah's prosperity made it a valuable target for a long series of invading powers. The remains of 18 historic fortresses, castles and towers testify to its turbulent history, with settlements occupied or challenged by the Sassanid Persians, the Islamic clans of the Arabian Gulf, and the Portuguese, Dutch and British colonial empires. History enthusiasts would welcome the chance to bring the past back to life during their visit to Ras Al Khaimah.

Working for the Sheikh, as my wife was now doing, yielded many benefits. The Sheikh is a brother to the ruler, His Highness Sheikh Saud bin Saqr al Qasimi. The school was for girls only. Sheikh Faisal bin Saqr al Qasimi was the owner; he wanted a school where his daughters could attend without mingling with boys. It was small but utterly unique.

His Highness Sheikh Saud was named Supreme Council Member and Ruler of Ras Al Khaimah on October 27, 2010, following the death of his father, His Highness Sheikh Saqr. Sheikh Saud's rule has meant a continuation of pro-growth policies which resulted in a per capita GDP increase of more than 50% from 2004 to 2007. In recent years, Ras Al Khaimah has continued to establish itself as a robust, growing market with a diversified economic base. Sheikh Saud studied economics at the University of Michigan and was instrumental in the founding and restructuring of some of the most successful corporate enterprises in Ras Al Khaimah: including Julphar Pharmaceuticals and RAK Ceramics.

For us, things seemed to be falling into place. We had started a building project in Zimbabwe which was now almost complete. The initial plan was for it to be a house; but given how big it turned out to be, we decided to turn it into a school. I am the project manager and did a great deal of research on how it could function as a school. I made all necessary applications to relevant ministries and the City Council. I also wrote a business proposal exploring the feasibility of the project. Funds permitting, we planned to open the school by January 2018.

We were in Ras Al Khaimah for two years when the employment contract came to an end and was not renewed. This news came suddenly, with no notice. It appears that the owners had got what they wanted after my wife had taken the school through accreditation. The news was devastating. We had no other plan, but God knew best.

Gallie made an application to one of the universities and secured a post. However, there was a delay in processing the paperwork; the wait was unbearable. When we finally received the necessary documentation, the start date was only three days later. We had to move very quickly to Fujairah. I remember us leaving everything behind, before moving to a hotel paid for by the new employer. We stayed there for 15 days. This was the beginning of yet another of our journeys.

## Fujairah

Moving to Fujairah would complete a triangle in our stay in the UAE. Gallie was to work for a very successful university, the Higher Colleges of Technology. She would be Manager of Academic Services, a powerful position within the leadership of the two colleges (male and female). I was content staying at home. In Fujairah, I accompanied my wife to retreats; it was a good start, which made us happy. At one of these retreats, Cove Rotana, I decided I would return to Zimbabwe to view the progress of our projects. Gallie normally came with me - but on this occasion, I had to go alone, for she had just started a new job. She agreed to this; in any other circumstance, she would have objected, because she was afraid for my safety alone in Zimbabwe.

Fujairah is an Emirate on the east coast of the UAE, lying along the Gulf of Oman. It's known for its beaches and the Hajar Mountains, which run through much of it. In the south, the city of Fujairah is home to the massive Sheikh Zayed Mosque, with its towering white minarets. Overlooking the city is Fujairah Fort, a reconstructed seventeenth century fortress, featuring a round and a square tower.

Dominated by the Sharqiyin tribe, Fujairah sits at the mouth of the important trade route, the Wadi Ham: guarded by the Sharqiyin Fort at Bithnah, it runs through the mountains to the interior and Persian Gulf Coast. Known as the Shamaliyah, the east coast of what is now the UAE was subject to Muscat until 1850, when it was annexed by the Al Qasim of Sharjah. It went on to frequently secede; and in 1901, Hamad bin Abdulla Al Sharqi, chief of the Sharqiyin, declared independence from Sharjah. This was recognised by a number of Trucial Sheikhs and by Muscat; but not the British, who were frequently provoked by the independently minded ruler.

Since the absorption of Kalba by Sharjah in 1952, the Shamaliyah is shared by the Emirates of Fujairah and Sharjah. In the same year, Fujairah entered into treaty relations with Britain, becoming the last Emirate to join the Trucial States. On 2 December 1971, Fujairah joined the UAE.

Fujairah is home to the oldest mosque in the UAE, built in 1446 from mud and bricks. It is similar to other mosques found in Yemen, eastern Oman, and Qatar. Al Bidyah Mosque has four domes (unlike similar mosques which have between seven and twelve), but lacks a minaret.

After our hotel stay, we moved to a villa in a quiet area in Al Faseel. This would be our home. Certainly, it very much felt that way when we slept there for the first time.

# CHAPTER 5:

# LOOKING BACK ON MY LIFE

In the eyes of my extended family and the society in which I grew up, what I have achieved in my life could be viewed as success. To me, though, real success means something else. It means fulfilling my potential in an atmosphere of happiness; and above all, being able to live each day at a time. I agree with William Bennett (1993: 225), who says, 'Happiness is like a cat. If you try to coax it, it will avoid you; it will never come. But if you pay no attention and go about your business, you'll find it rubbing against your legs and jumping into your lap'. From these wise words, I have learnt that the happy man is not he who seems thus to others, but he who seems thus to himself.

Soon after Zimbabwean independence, I bought a house in what had been a no-go area during colonial times. I had cars and life appeared rosy. Things began to change for the worse due to economic hardship. The certificates, diplomas and all the assets I had did not seem to work. Eventually, I suffered a total collapse of morale and motivation. I could not get promoted, could not feed my family in a decent way, and recalled my father's teaching that a man who failed to feed his children was worse than nothing.

It was my wife's idea that we try something else. She suggested pursuing higher and further education: which worked. This reminded me of my grandfather - who taught us that when one door of happiness closes, another one opens, but we often look so long at the closed door that we do not see the one which has opened for us. I go by the words of Michel De Montaigne (2003: 114): 'The pleasantest things in the world are pleasant thoughts; and the art of life is to have as many as possible'.

When I look back at my childhood, and the difficulties I faced especially in my early years of school, I truly appreciate that to obtain a proper education, someone must be highly motivated and dedicated. Yet exactly how I managed to forge ahead despite the adversity I have experienced is still a mystery to me. One reason could be that I am the sort of person who cannot settle for less. I am adventurous and capable of thriving in dramatic situations and challenges. One day, out of sheer curiosity, I followed a spitting cobra. I did the unthinkable that day. Snakes are very flexible; on entering their den, they coil and push their body down the hole, while the head comes out. The cobra entered the hole and out came its head. I was lucky to avoid the spirts as I ran for dear life.

The other reason I was so resilient is I am the sort of person who does not complain much or blame anybody for my misfortunes. I carry on looking for solutions. The struggle for education is everybody's responsibility; not influenced by anything other than motivation and discipline. I understand the role played by a conducive environment to learning; but the learner should be able to navigate themselves through difficulty before realising any goals. What I have achieved is a product of hard work and the need to move on and achieve my goals.

That said, I can also see now that according to the 'functionalist perspective' (Giddens 2000), my society acted as an institution to ensure continuity. Viewed through this prism, the family performs important tasks which contribute to society's basic needs; and helps perpetuate social order. For example, even though some members of my family sometimes forgot me, my brother always came to my rescue when things looked unfavourable. Yet it was only later that my family realised the need to educate us.

The death of my father brings back a lot of sad memories. I still have problems coming to terms with what happened. I went to see him during the August school holidays. I remember giving him ten pence. He was going away from home to receive treatment that time, so I did not have much time to see him. We parted ways and that was it. I was told that he had passed no more a week after he had been buried. Had it not been for my friend telephoning the school principal, I might have only heard about his death fully three months later.

I experienced very similar pain when my mother passed away. At the time of writing this, I have still not been to her resting place. I have a profound feeling of loss which is difficult to explain. It is a strange feeling which cannot be satisfied until I see where she is.

Changes have slowly occurred in Zimbabwean society during my life. More and more families began to see the need to be literate; more and more girls were sent to school. Feminist ideologies did not exist 50 years ago in my country, but women did have rights. They were entitled to their proper place as mothers, sisters and aunts. Moreover, in their own capacity, women in my community have tried to assert themselves in various ways: such as singing lullabies and naming their children or dogs in a connotative way.

However, especially in my working life, and particularly in the UK, I have learned that men and women are affected by gender stereotypes in one way or another. I agree with Faludi (1999) that 'the idea that man dominates is a myth'. Even though some groups of men are still confident and feel in control, many others find themselves marginalised and lacking in respect. When we were growing up as boys, we had to meet these challenges of 'masculinity' in fights and feats of bravery. As a result, we were not allowed to weep or shed tears in public. Any signs of weakness were categorised as feminine.

Back in the 1960s and early 1970s, things for the ordinary Zimbabwean remained tough, with huge struggles in getting enough food, children into school and travelling around. There were droughts, but AIDS had not yet arrived to wreak its awful destruction. The satisfying thing was that most people were content with whatever they did. There was no significant violence on the streets; the villages were a perfect sanctuary for holidaymakers. I used to go home every school holiday to try and improve the lives of my own family and till the land to make surplus food available. My salary could not meet the needs of the family, and I'd been given the task of educating my brother's children. Yet life was enjoyable even without resources.

The advent of AIDS, however, claimed many, young and old. Initially, people thought it was a form of witchcraft on those who had committed adultery with someone else's wife. Many went to different witch doctors to find a cure. Ignorance has no defence. People died in their thousands; very few families were not affected by the pandemic. People from my age group and those born in the 1960s were worst affected. At cemeteries on a daily basis, different groups of people could be seen burying their dead.

Those who had not taken this seriously surely had to rethink - yet some simply refused to do so. Some silent carriers of the virus continued to go around spreading the disease, convinced they were safe. This created havoc: by the time they were discovered to be causing the problem, the damage was already done, and many had perished. The AIDS pandemic is a story worth telling on its own. It was and remains a menace to African society. In Uganda, a whole generation was wiped out by the disease.

The education system in Zimbabwe has a long history of disadvantaging the poor, especially the rural poor. A great deal of credit must go to Christian organisations which helped educate the masses. Some of them trained teachers, nurses and doctors. No politician or successful individual in Zimbabwe does not owe everything to the Christian sector. I came through this window of opportunity in this way. I went to a Salvation Army School (1958-1968) for my primary education; then enrolled at Mazowe Salvation Army Secondary School (1969-1972); then trained at Waddilove Teacher Training College, a Methodist establishment (1974-1976).

From my primary education through to teacher training, I encountered a series of problems encompassing failure to obtain fees, food, accommodation, or support from my family. In some cases, I had to remain in the school to work and raise school fees. When my parents could not raise fees for my Standard 4 to 6, I left home; quite an adventure for an 11-year-old. Yet through my own determination and resourcefulness, and with the help of others, I made it, learning lessons and skills which would last me a lifetime.

## Political philosophy

In my memoirs, I want to embrace my own philosophies of life, shaped by my upbringing, my life experiences and my Christian view on what I have observed in this world. I was born into a society ruled by the British, who had colonised our land and dispossessed our forefathers. I have researched what happened when my ancestors first met the white man. They had formerly lived in the Nenguwo/Nyandoro area (known as Marondera today). On hearing that the white man was advancing to what is now northern Zimbabwe, they headed in the direction of Shamva. This is where they met Pari, a white man who made them pay him for seeing him and for his protection. This was their first poll tax; a guarantee they would not be harassed by the Ndebele raids.

This background dominates my ideas about life and existence. We grew up learning that the white man was supreme, untouchable and always the boss. This imposed fear in the most real sense and is entrenched in present day Zimbabwe. Indeed, I feel that the ghost of the white man still possesses our society even now. The greatest problem is it has been inherited by some elite black people, who now own vast wealth which they will not share with the general public. They make a lot of money at the expense of the state coffers; and drain the economy while claiming that they fought for and liberated the country.

As I grew up, there was general discontent about the state of things. We were politicised into realising that our very existence depended upon land where we could build our homes and graze our cattle; where we could hunt for everything that could make our lives worthy. I do not know whether to blame President Mugabe and his earlier policies of land acquisition and dispossessing the white man. People in Zimbabwe today have varying ideas and suggestions about land. Could we say that what happened was for the best? I supported it; I still support the idea even now. But what I criticise is the greedy, so-called black white man (Varungu Vatema).

# EPILOGUE:

# BLESSING PROMOTED TO GLORY

*This is where Blessing ended the story of his life before death tragically claimed him. He was 63 when he died of a stroke in Fujairah, UAE, on 14 April 2017. As an epilogue to his story, which he had not finished, a poem, written by his nephew, will conclude the life of a gentle giant. It is called 'Blessing promoted to glory'.*

The nephew of Blessing, from the heart speaks;
God gives life and it is Him who gives in abundance,
Yet today we mourn the passing on of our hero
For his life on earth has come to night
Silently, swiftly without warning or expectation,

He is gone, he who was a friend to all,
Resting now on Abraham bosom at starry heights,
On promotion to heavenly glory
And we sing and dance in triumphal jubilation
Celebrating the life of a soldier of Salvation,

A great warrior, he has fought a good fight of faith

With a pure heart and a heart of gold,
In his absence days are dull and the future is bleak,
Now we bury him armed, with his weapons of war;
He sleeps sublime among the flowers of the garden,

Rest in peace our most cherished Blessing,
A father to many, and a teacher to many more,
Your loving family; wife, children, siblings and all
Will miss your love and your words of wisdom,
You have gone and now you live in our hearts.

-    *Thomas Chidavaenzi (nephew), 2017*

# REFERENCES

Achebe, C. (1959). *Things Fall Apart.* New York: Everyman's Library.

Bennett, W. (1993). *The Book of Virtues: A Treasury of Great Moral Stories.* New York: Simon & Schuster.

Boyter, M. (n.d.). *Memorygrabber Life Story Workbook.* eBook available from: http://www.familyhistoryproducts.com/memorygrabber.html

Dangarembwa, T. *Nervous_Conditions.* New York: Seal Press.

De Montaigne, M. (2003). *The Complete Essays.* London: Penguin Books.

Faludi, S. (1999). *Stiffed: The Betrayal of the Modern Man.* London: Chatto & Windus.

Frank, A. (2002). Why study people's stories? The dialogical ethics of narrative analysis. *International Journal of Qualitative Methods*, 1 (1), Article 6.

Gardner, H. (1993). *Multiple Intelligences: The Theory in Practice.* New York: Basic Books.

Giddens, A. (2000). *Runaway World: How Globalisation is Reshaping Our Lives.* London: Profile Books.

McLeod, J. (2001). *Qualitative Research in Counselling and Psychotherapy.* Thousand Oaks, CA: Sage Publications.

Walby, S. (1990). *Theorizing Patriarchy.* Oxford: Basil Blackwell